The Death Penalty

Other Books of Related Interest:

Opposing Viewpoints Series

Interracial America

At Issue Series

Alternative Prisons

Guns and Crime

Introducing Issues with Opposing Viewpoints

Gangs

Torture

"Congress shall make no law ... abridging the freedom of speech, or of the press."

First Amendment to the US Constitution

The basic foundation of our democracy is the First Amendment guarantee of freedom of expression. The Opposing Viewpoints series is dedicated to the concept of this basic freedom and the idea that it is more important to practice it than to enshrine it.

The Death Penalty

Jenny Cromie and Lynn M. Zott, Book Editors

GREENHAVEN PRESS
A part of Gale, Cengage Learning

Detroit • New York • San Francisco • New Haven, Conn • Waterville, Maine • London

Elizabeth Des Chenes, *Director, Publishing Solutions*

© 2013 Greenhaven Press, a part of Gale, Cengage Learning.

Gale and Greenhaven Press are registered trademarks used herein under license.

For more information, contact:
Greenhaven Press
27500 Drake Rd.
Farmington Hills, MI 48331-3535
Or you can visit our Internet site at gale.cengage.com

For product information and technology assistance, contact us at

Gale Customer Support, 1-800-877-4253
For permission to use material from this text or product, submit all requests online at www.cengage.com/permissions

Further permissions questions can be emailed to permissionrequest@cengage.com

Articles in Greenhaven Press anthologies are often edited for length to meet page requirements. In addition, original titles of these works are changed to clearly present the main thesis and to explicitly indicate the author's opinion. Every effort is made to ensure that Greenhaven Press accurately reflects the original intent of the authors. Every effort has been made to trace the owners of copyrighted material.

Cover Image copyright © Thinkstock/Getty Images.

LIBRARY OF CONGRESS CATALOGING-IN-PUBLICATION DATA

The death penalty / Jenny Cromie and Lynn M. Zott, book editors.
    p. cm. -- (Opposing viewpoints)
    Includes bibliographical references and index.
    ISBN 978-0-7377-4960-1 (hardcover) -- ISBN 978-0-7377-4961-8 (pbk.)
    1. Capital punishment--United States. I. Cromie, Jenny. II. Zott, Lynn M. (Lynn Marie), 1969-
    HV8699.U5D343 2012
    364.660973--dc23

                            2012021471

Printed in the United States of America
1 2 3 4 5 6 7 16 15 14 13 12

Contents

Chapter 3: Is the Death Penalty Applied Fairly?

Chapter 4: Should the Death Penalty Be Abolished or Reformed?

Why Consider Opposing Viewpoints?

> *"The only way in which a human being can make some approach to knowing the whole of a subject is by hearing what can be said about it by persons of every variety of opinion and studying all modes in which it can be looked at by every character of mind. No wise man ever acquired his wisdom in any mode but this."*
>
> *John Stuart Mill*

In our media-intensive culture it is not difficult to find differing opinions. Thousands of newspapers and magazines and dozens of radio and television talk shows resound with differing points of view. The difficulty lies in deciding which opinion to agree with and which "experts" seem the most credible. The more inundated we become with differing opinions and claims, the more essential it is to hone critical reading and thinking skills to evaluate these ideas. Opposing Viewpoints books address this problem directly by presenting stimulating debates that can be used to enhance and teach these skills. The varied opinions contained in each book examine many different aspects of a single issue. While examining these conveniently edited opposing views, readers can develop critical thinking skills such as the ability to compare and contrast authors' credibility, facts, argumentation styles, use of persuasive techniques, and other stylistic tools. In short, the Opposing Viewpoints Series is an ideal way to attain the higher-level thinking and reading skills so essential in a culture of diverse and contradictory opinions.

In addition to providing a tool for critical thinking, Opposing Viewpoints books challenge readers to question their own strongly held opinions and assumptions. Most people form their opinions on the basis of upbringing, peer pressure, and personal, cultural, or professional bias. By reading carefully balanced opposing views, readers must directly confront new ideas as well as the opinions of those with whom they disagree. This is not to argue simplistically that everyone who reads opposing views will—or should—change his or her opinion. Instead, the series enhances readers' understanding of their own views by encouraging confrontation with opposing ideas. Careful examination of others' views can lead to the readers' understanding of the logical inconsistencies in their own opinions, perspective on why they hold an opinion, and the consideration of the possibility that their opinion requires further evaluation.

Evaluating Other Opinions

To ensure that this type of examination occurs, Opposing Viewpoints books present all types of opinions. Prominent spokespeople on different sides of each issue as well as well-known professionals from many disciplines challenge the reader. An additional goal of the series is to provide a forum for other, less known, or even unpopular viewpoints. The opinion of an ordinary person who has had to make the decision to cut off life support from a terminally ill relative, for example, may be just as valuable and provide just as much insight as a medical ethicist's professional opinion. The editors have two additional purposes in including these less known views. One, the editors encourage readers to respect others' opinions—even when not enhanced by professional credibility. It is only by reading or listening to and objectively evaluating others' ideas that one can determine whether they are worthy of consideration. Two, the inclusion of such viewpoints encourages the important critical thinking skill of objectively evaluating an author's credentials and bias. This evaluation will illuminate an author's reasons for taking a particular stance on an issue and will aid in readers' evaluation of the author's ideas.

It is our hope that these books will give readers a deeper understanding of the issues debated and an appreciation of the complexity of even seemingly simple issues when good and honest people disagree. This awareness is particularly important in a democratic society such as ours in which people enter into public debate to determine the common good. Those with whom one disagrees should not be regarded as enemies but rather as people whose views deserve careful examination and may shed light on one's own.

Thomas Jefferson once said that "difference of opinion leads to inquiry, and inquiry to truth." Jefferson, a broadly educated man, argued that "if a nation expects to be ignorant and free . . . it expects what never was and never will be." As individuals and as a nation, it is imperative that we consider the opinions of others and examine them with skill and discernment. The Opposing Viewpoints series is intended to help readers achieve this goal.

David L. Bender and Bruno Leone,
Founders

Introduction

> *"A system that takes life must first give justice."*
>
> —*John J. Curtin Jr.,*
> *former American Bar*
> *Association president*

Troy Davis—who maintained his innocence until his September 21, 2011, execution—was put to death by lethal injection for the 1989 murder of an off-duty police officer in Savannah, Georgia. His execution, which touched off outrage and a worldwide firestorm of debate about the US death penalty system, proceeded after being postponed more than three hours while the US Supreme Court considered a last-minute stay of execution. His execution also moved forward despite calls for clemency from former Federal Bureau of Investigation (FBI) director and judge William S. Sessions, Pope Benedict XVI, former president Jimmy Carter, Archbishop Desmond Tutu, fifty-one members of the US Congress, and numerous others. In addition, nearly one million people signed petitions on Davis's behalf, urging the Georgia State Board of Pardons and Paroles to grant Davis clemency.

The Supreme Court's decision and Georgia's criminal justice system drew sharp criticism for what many viewed as a miscarriage of justice. Disturbing to many was what appeared to be corruption of justice in Davis's case—namely, reports of alleged police misconduct and coercion of witnesses, seven of nine key witnesses recanting all or part of their testimony against him, and reports that someone else had confessed to the crime. Despite this information, state and federal judges refused to grant Davis a new trial.

Davis's long walk to execution began in 1991 when he was convicted of killing an off-duty police officer by the name of

Mark MacPhail, who was working as a security guard at the time. According to prosecutors, MacPhail was shot as he rushed to help a homeless man. Prosecutors said Davis was hitting the homeless man with a handgun, and that he later shot MacPhail in a Burger King parking lot. While no gun was ever found in connection with the shooting, prosecutors had maintained during the trial that shell casings found near the crime scene were linked to an earlier shooting involving Davis. However, ballistics evidence later showed that no such link existed between Davis and the previous shooting.

In a September 15, 2011, *Atlanta Journal-Constitution* editorial, former FBI director William S. Sessions wrote that an evidentiary hearing in Davis's case revealed some disturbing information. "What the hearing demonstrated most conclusively was that the evidence in this case—consisting almost entirely of conflicting stories, testimonies and statements—is inadequate to the task of convincingly establishing either Davis' guilt or his innocence. Without DNA or other forms of physical or scientific evidence that can be objectively measured and tested, it is possible that doubts about guilt in this case will never be resolved. However, when it comes to the sentence of death, there should be no room for doubt." Sessions went on to say that there is no more serious crime than the murder of a police officer, but he added that "justice is not done for Officer Mark Allen MacPhail Sr. if the wrong man is punished." In the editorial, Sessions further urged that Davis not be executed, but rather sentenced to life.

Others who reviewed the case were not convinced of Davis's innocence, but were nonetheless disturbed by the way the case was handled and the questions that it raised about the death penalty system itself. One day prior to Davis's execution, Jay Bookman—editorial writer for the *Atlanta Journal-Constitution*—wrote that while he did not believe that Davis was innocent of the crime, "there is no DNA evidence in the case, no fingerprint evidence, to substantiate that fact.

The case is based almost entirely on testimony from eyewitnesses that in some instances has altered over the passage of time." Bookman did not advocate that Davis be freed, but he asserted that "the sense of closure and justice that would be provided to some by his execution does not outweigh the possibility that we would be compounding one tragic killing by committing another."

Three years after Davis's conviction and years before the details of Davis's case would play out in the US criminal justice system, the late Supreme Court justice Harry A. Blackmun wrote a dissenting opinion in a 1994 case, *Callins v. Collins*, that sparked some debate about the death penalty as an institution. The case was an appeal by a Texas inmate that the Supreme Court refused to hear. In his lone dissenting opinion, Blackmun wrote: "From this day forward, I no longer shall tinker with the machinery of death. . . . [T]he death penalty experiment has failed." Blackmun said it was time that the Supreme Court abandon the "delusion" that capital punishment could ever be consistent with the US Constitution. He also stated in media interviews that he had doubts whether the court system could administer the death penalty fairly. Eighty-five years old at the time he wrote his now-famous dissenting opinion, Blackmun said he believed the Supreme Court would ultimately reach the same conclusion about capital punishment—an institution he admitted to struggling with for twenty years. "I may not live to see that day," he said, "but I have faith that eventually it will arrive."

Blackmun died in 1999—twelve years prior to Davis's execution. What he would have written in the aftermath of Davis's case is difficult to say. However, following the *Callins v. Collins* case, Blackmun said: "It seems that the decision whether a human being should live or die is so inherently subjective—rife with all of life's understanding, experiences, prejudices, and passions—that it inevitably defies the rationality and consistency required by the Constitution."

While some have continued to debate Davis's innocence, public discourse about capital punishment and the US death penalty system reached a new level following his September 2011 execution. Independent of the Davis case, many states already were considering various issues related to capital punishment. As of mid-2012, there were thirty-three states that still allowed the death penalty. But an increasing number are taking a closer look at the punishment, with some considering reform and others contemplating an outright repeal of the institution altogether. On April 25, 2012, Connecticut became the seventeenth state to abolish the death penalty. On a global scale, the tide of public opinion also seems to be shifting, with more than two-thirds of countries abolishing the death penalty in recent years.

With death penalty cases costing as much as $1 to $3 million, many financially strapped state governments are considering the cost alone as reason to change course. Beyond financial concerns, however, debates about the death penalty usually hit a number of hot-button issues that touch on religious views, racism, human rights, ethics, morality, and the value that society places on life itself.

Discussions about capital punishment often produce thought-provoking—and sometimes disturbing—questions that individuals and society are compelled to answer. But as with many other controversial issues, answers to those questions are not always easy to come by, and the solutions themselves often raise equally troubling questions. The following chapters of *Opposing Viewpoints: The Death Penalty*—Is the Death Penalty Just and Ethical?, Does the Death Penalty Serve the Public Good?, Is the Death Penalty Applied Fairly?, and Should the Death Penalty Be Abolished or Reformed?—explore the full range of issues surrounding the death penalty system. The authors of the viewpoints provide insight into some of the more common controversies and questions surrounding capital punishment as an institution in the United States.

OPPOSING
VIEWPOINTS®
SERIES

CHAPTER 1

Is the Death Penalty Just and Ethical?

Chapter Preface

Few issues—except perhaps abortion—seem to divide people as much as the death penalty; at the heart of both issues is life itself.

When someone takes the life of an innocent, law-abiding citizen, should that person's life be taken in return as the ultimate punishment? Some say that taking a life is wrong, whether it is done through the death penalty or murder. Included in this camp are those individuals and organizations—like Amnesty International—who believe that answering violence with capital punishment is a barbaric solution in an otherwise civilized society.

By administering the death penalty to society's worst offenders, the criminal justice system itself commits human rights abuses, according to Amnesty International. The organization argues, "The death penalty is the ultimate, irreversible denial of human rights. It is the premeditated and cold-blooded killing of a human being by the state. It violates the right to life as proclaimed in the Universal Declaration of Human Rights, and the right to be free from cruel, inhuman and degrading punishment."

On the other side of the debate are those who believe that failing to answer the worst offenders with the strongest punishment available sends the wrong message about the value that society places on human life. In fact, some argue that in a civilized society, the death penalty is a necessary evil to protect innocent people from the most dangerous criminals in society. Some also argue that murderers forfeit their rights—including their right to life—at the time that they commit the crime.

The debate about capital punishment contains complicated questions with few simple answers. While the death penalty is considered legal in some states, many consider it an unethical, immoral, and unjust response to society's worst criminal acts. As a moral compass, many look to religion for answers; others look to the legal system. Still others rely on a sense of what is right and ethical based on the guidance of various secular organizations and authorities. One thing is clear, however: The tide of public opinion appears to be changing where capital punishment is concerned.

Worldwide, there were 527 executions in 2010, down from 714 in 2009—a 25 percent decline, according to Amnesty International. In addition, more than two-thirds of the countries in the world have abolished the death penalty in law, or in practice, in recent years. As of April 2011, ninety-five countries had abolished it—including most of Europe. Other countries have the death penalty on record as a permissible punishment but do not use it. Despite these worldwide shifts, the United States was ranked fifth in the number of executions carried out in 2010, with a total of forty-six, according to Amnesty International. Other countries with the most executions worldwide in 2010 included China, Iran, Saudi Arabia, and Yemen.

Statistics aside, the debate about whether the death penalty is just and ethical is likely to continue as states and individuals examine the institution of capital punishment. In recent years, an increasing number of states have started to take a closer look at their death penalty statutes, with an eye toward reform or abolishment of the institution altogether. In the United States, seventeen states have abolished the death penalty, with Connecticut the most recent state to do so in April 2012.

In the following chapter, authors of the viewpoints examine some of the issues surrounding the death penalty debate, highlighting arguments related to religious views; medical ethics; human rights; and what it means to live in a just, civilized society.

> *"Putting aside deterrence, supporters emphasize a second reason for continuing the death penalty: Society needs to show its moral outrage at particularly heinous crimes."*

Why I Support the Death Penalty

Edward Koch

In the following viewpoint, Edward Koch claims his support for the death penalty. Koch does not believe that there has been an incident where an innocent person has been put to death. He acknowledges that innocent men and women have been convicted in trial, but as a result of appeals, they have been exonerated. He concludes optimistic that scholars who support the death penalty will speak out and counter the opponents' arguments. Edward Koch served as mayor of New York from 1978 to 1989.

As you read, consider the following questions:

1. Who is Edward Koch, according to the viewpoint?

2. How many states retain the death penalty, according to Koch?

3. According to a Gallup poll, how many Americans still support the death penalty?

A *New York Times* editorial on April 27 continued the paper's ongoing campaign over the years to end the death penalty in the United States.

The editorial points out that only 33 states retain the death penalty. New York is not one of them. Wikipedia notes how that came to be. It reports:

> "*People v. LaValle*, 3 N.Y.3d 88 (2004), was a landmark decision by the New York Court of Appeals, the highest court in the U.S. state of New York, in which the court ruled that the state's death penalty statute was unconstitutional because of the statute's direction on how the jury was to be instructed in case of deadlock. New York has since been without the death penalty, as the law has not been amended."

The *Times* cites a recent report issued by the National Research Council, which "has now reached the striking and convincing conclusion that all of the research about deterrence and the death penalty done in the past generation, including by some first-rank scholars at the most prestigious universities, should be ignored."

Why?

The *Times* editorial continued, "A lot of the research assumes that 'potential murderers respond to the objective risk of execution,' but only one in six of the people sentenced to death in the last 35 years have been executed and no study properly took that diminished risk into account."

Is it reasonable to believe that potential murderers were aware of the statistic that most death penalty sentences were not being carried out? I, having a scholarly interest in the topic, was not aware of this fact.

Putting aside deterrence, supporters emphasize a second reason for continuing the death penalty: Society needs to show its moral outrage at particularly heinous crimes, such as the one committed in Connecticut in July 2007. That crime involved the brutal raping of a 48-year-old woman and one of

Society Has the Right to Prevent Future Crimes

It cheapens the life of an innocent murder victim to say that society has no right to keep the murderer from ever killing again.

Steven D. Stewart,
"A Message from the Prosecuting Attorney,"
Office of the Clark County Prosecuting Attorney, 2009.
www.clarkprosecutor.org.

her daughters. Both daughters, one 17 years old, and the other 11 years old, were tied to their beds and perished when their house was set on fire.

The two men, apprehended and convicted of the crimes in separate trials, were sentenced to death. Last week Connecticut's Gov. Dannel Malloy signed a law abolishing the death penalty in that state.

Amazingly, after the incessant campaign by death penalty opponents, an October 2011 Gallup poll showed that 61 percent of Americans still support the penalty, down from an all-time high of 80 percent in 1994.

I remain one of those who support the death penalty and, as of this moment in time, the U.S. Supreme Court's decision finding the death penalty constitutional remains the law of the land.

I do not believe there is a single case in the U.S. where academics and law enforcement authorities agree that an innocent person has been put to death. Yes, innocent people have been convicted at trial, but as a result of appeals, they have been exonerated before the sentence was carried out.

Even if opponents were to cite such a case, I would still support having the penalty available as an option in particularly heinous murders. The reason being that many more innocent lives would be saved because of the deterrence factor.

Death penalty opponents always claim racism in the meting out of the penalty, conveying that blacks and Hispanics are victims of that racism. What they rarely state is that while proportionate to the population, whites commit fewer murders than blacks and Hispanics, they receive the death penalty in greater numbers.

The cry of racism by the opponents really stems from the contention that the murderers of minority victims are given prison sentences to a greater degree than death sentences, whereas the murderers of white victims are more likely to be given death sentences.

Those opponents don't urge that more minority murderers of minorities be given the death penalty in larger numbers upon conviction, but rather that no one suffer that penalty.

Also, did anyone at the *Times* editorial board consider what the effect on the murder rate in the U.S. might be if instead of one in six executions being carried out, six in six were timely executed and reported on the front pages of the *Times* and other papers?

Death penalty opponents certainly have the right to express their views as they have successfully done for many years, causing a reduction in support for the penalty.

Regrettably, their editorials have frightened many in the public from speaking out in favor of retaining the death penalty for fear of being labeled racist when such a charge is manifestly unfair. I hope those "first-rank scholars at the most prestigious universities" supporting the death penalty (I don't recall the *Times* referring to their opinions in its prior editorials) will now speak out.

I also hope that other death penalty supporters get involved in this discussion. Don't be frightened into silence.

> "A society that turns its back on redemption commits itself to holding on to anger and a need for vengeance in a quest for fulfillment that cannot be met by those destructive emotions."

Justice Is Not Served with the Death Penalty

Raymond Lesniak

Raymond Lesniak is a Democratic state senator from New Jersey and author of The Road to Abolition: How New Jersey Abolished the Death Penalty. *In the following viewpoint, he argues that the death penalty violates basic human rights. Using several examples, Lesniak also points out that the death penalty has led to the execution of innocent people, and that it adds to the suffering experienced by victims' families. According to Lesniak, the death penalty damages society as a whole because it encourages revenge over redemption, leading to hate and violence. There is even evidence, Lesniak asserts, that death penalty executions increase murder rates.*

As you read, consider the following questions:

1. According to Lesniak, how many human beings are awaiting execution in the United States?

2. How many wrongfully convicted death row inmates does Lesniak say have been released since 1973?

3. What reason was given for the stoning death of a thirteen-year-old girl in Somalia, according to Lesniak?

I come here today [February 2, 2009] not to plead a case for a victim whose fundamental human rights have been violated. But, rather, to plead the case that the death penalty violates the fundamental human rights of mankind. In my country, the United States of America, over 3,000 human beings are awaiting execution, some for a crime they did not commit. I plead the case that the death penalty in the United States, Iraq, Pakistan, Japan, wherever, exposes the innocent to execution, causes more suffering to the family members of murder victims, serves no penal purpose and commits society to the belief that revenge is preferable to redemption.

On December 17, 2007, New Jersey became the first state in the Union to abolish the death penalty since the U.S. Supreme Court reinstated it in 1976. When Governor Jon Corzine signed the legislation I sponsored into law, he also commuted the death sentences of eight human beings. The Community of Sant'Egidio in Rome, Italy, a lay Catholic organization committed to abolishing the death penalty throughout the world, lit up the Roman Coliseum to celebrate this victory for human rights.

How was this victory achieved? First, by demonstrating that the death penalty creates the possibility of executing an innocent human being. One of our founding founders, Benjamin Franklin, quoting the British jurist William Blackstone, said: "It's better to let 100 guilty men go free than to imprison an innocent person." Yet Governor Corzine and my legislation let no guilty person go free. It merely replaced the death penalty with life without parole, eliminating the possibility of putting to death an innocent human being.

An Innocent Man Is Set Free and a Killer Is Brought to Justice

Byron Halsey could have been one such human being. On July 9, 2007, Byron walked out of jail a free man after serving 19 years in prison for a most heinous crime: the murder of a seven-year-old girl and an eight-year-old boy. Both had been sexually assaulted; the girl was strangled to death, and nails were driven into the boy's head.

Halsey, who had a sixth-grade education and severe learning disabilities, was interrogated for 30 hours shortly after the children's bodies were discovered. He confessed to the murders and, even though his statement was factually inaccurate as to the location of the bodies and the manner of death, his confession was admitted into evidence in a court of law. The prosecution sought the death penalty.

Halsey was convicted of two counts of felony murder and one count of aggravated sexual assault. He was sentenced to two life terms: narrowly evading the death penalty by the vote of one juror who held out against it during the sentencing portion of his trial.

After spending nearly half his life behind bars, post-trial DNA analysis determined, with scientific certainty, that Byron did not commit the murders. A witness for the prosecution at his trial is now accused of those crimes.

But for the good judgment of that one juror, Mr. Halsey might have been executed, and the real killer would never have been discovered and brought to justice.

Many Innocents Will Be Executed

Stories like Byron's are not uncommon. Since 1973, 130 human beings on death rows throughout the United States have been released from jail for being wrongfully convicted. During that time, over 1,100 prisoners were executed. How many of them were innocent? 3,309 remain on death row throughout the U.S. How many of them are innocent? How many of the innocent will be executed?

It could be Troy Davis. He's been imprisoned since 1989 in the state of Georgia for a murder he maintains he did not commit. In one of Davis's numerous appeals, the chief justice of the Georgia Supreme Court said, "In this case, nearly every witness who identified Davis as the shooter at trial has now disclaimed his or her ability to do so reliably. Three persons have stated that Sylvester Coles confessed to being the shooter." Coles had testified against Davis at the trial.

On September 23, 2008, less than two hours before Davis was due to be put to death by lethal injection, he received a stay of execution by the US Supreme Court. On October 14 the stay was lifted and the state of Georgia issued an execution warrant for October 27. Three days before this execution date, the 11th Circuit Court stayed the execution to consider a new appeal.

Will Troy Davis be the next innocent person saved from execution, or will he be the next innocent person executed? [Editor's note: Troy Davis was executed by lethal injection on September 21, 2011.]

The Death Penalty Offers No Consolation to Victims' Families

Does the death penalty serve any purpose, other than to do harm to everyone involved, and society in general? Does the death penalty even console the families of murder victims?

Not according to 63 family members of murder victims who stated in a letter to the New Jersey legislature:

> We are family members and loved ones of murder victims. We desperately miss the parents, children, siblings, and spouses we have lost. We live with the pain and heartbreak of their absence every day and would do anything to have

them back. We have been touched by the criminal justice system in ways we never imagined and would never wish on anyone. Our experience compels us to speak out for change. Though we share different perspectives on the death penalty, every one of us agrees that New Jersey's capital punishment system doesn't work, and that our state is better off without it.

Or more specifically stated by Vicki Schieber whose daughter, Shannon, was raped and murdered, "The death penalty is a harmful policy that exacerbates the pain for murdered victims' families."

The Jury Is Still Out on the Deterrent Effect of the Death Penalty

Some argue that the death penalty is a deterrent to murder, yet more than a dozen studies published in the past 10 years have been inconclusive on its deterrent effect.

In testimony before the Subcommittee on the Constitution, Civil Rights and [Human] Rights of the United States Senate Judiciary Committee in February 2006, Richard [C.] Dieter, executive director of the Death Penalty Information Center, testified that states without a death penalty statute have significantly lower murder rates than their counterparts with the death penalty. Mr. Dieter also testified that of the four geographic regions in the U.S., the South, which carries out 80% of all executions in the country, has the highest murder rate. Conversely, the Northeast, which implements less than 1% of all executions, has the lowest murder rate in the nation.

Even those who believe the death penalty can act as a deterrent admit that existing research has inconclusive results. Professor Erik Lillquist of Seton Hall University School of Law testified that recent econometric studies conclude that the death penalty can act as a deterrent, but only if the death penalty is implemented in a "sufficient" number of cases. Conversely, he also maintained that other studies suggest that executions can cause a "brutalization effect," in which the murder rate actually increases.

Professor Lillquist stated:

> It just may be impossible to know what the deterrent or brutalization effect is here . . . at least as an empirical matter—simply because we're never going to have a large enough database that can be removed from the confounding variables, such that we can come to a conclusion. When scientists run studies in general, we try to do it in a controlled environment. You can't do that with murders and the death penalty.

Jeffrey [A.] Fagan, professor of law and public health, Columbia University, and Steven Durlauf . . . professor of economics, University of Wisconsin-Madison, wrote in a letter to the editor in the *Philadelphia Enquirer* on November 17, 2007:

> Serious researchers studying the death penalty continue to find that the relationship between executions and homicides is fragile and complex, inconsistent across the states, and highly sensitive to different research strategies. The only scientifically and ethically acceptable conclusion from the complete body of existing social science literature on deterrence and the death penalty is that it's impossible to tell whether deterrent effects are strong or weak, or whether they exist at all.

The professors concluded:

> Until research survives the rigors of replication and thorough testing of alternative hypotheses and sound impartial peer review, it provides no basis for decisions to take lives.

The Death Penalty Breeds a Culture of Revenge

While the death penalty inevitably executes the innocent, exacerbates the pain and suffering of families of murder victims

The Death Penalty Is a Violation of Human Rights

No matter what reason a government gives for executing prisoners and what method of execution is used, the death penalty cannot be separated from the issue of human rights. The movement for abolition cannot be separated from the movement for human rights. . . .

There can never be a justification for torture or for cruel, inhumane or degrading treatment or punishment. The cruelty of the death penalty is evident. Like torture, an execution constitutes an extreme physical and mental assault on a person already rendered helpless by government authorities.

"The Death Penalty v. Human Rights:
Why Abolish the Death Penalty?," Amnesty International,
September 2007. www.amnesty.org.

and serves no penal purpose, the worse damage it does is to a society that believes it needs to seek revenge over redemption.

The need for revenge leads to hate and violence. Redemption opens the door to healing and peace. Revenge slams it shut.

A society that turns its back on redemption commits itself to holding on to anger and a need for vengeance in a quest for fulfillment that cannot be met by those destructive emotions. Redemption instead opens the door to the space that asks healing questions in the wake of violence: questions of crime prevention; questions of why some human beings put such a low value on life that they readily take it from others; questions that help us understand how to help those impacted by violence; questions that take a back seat, and are often ignored, when our minds and emotions are filled with a need for revenge.

Thirty-six states and the federal government of the United States still [early 2009] impose the death penalty. The United States has more human beings in prison and more violence than just about every other civilized country in the world. As long as we continue to choose revenge over redemption, it's likely we will continue to be a leader in the amount of violence and size of our prison population.

It doesn't have to stay that way.

There Is a Link Between Violence and the Death Penalty

When New Jersey abolished its death penalty, it chose redemption over revenge, healing over hate, peace over war. We need more states and our federal government to make those same choices. Consider the following headlines which appeared side by side in the *New York Times*: "Iraqi Leaders Say the Way Is Clear for the Execution of 'Chemical Ali.'" The other headline read: "Bomber at Funeral Kills Dozens in Pakistan."

Both Iraq and Pakistan have the death penalty. After the announcement setting the execution date for "Chemical Ali" [Ali Hassan al-Majid, former Iraqi government official, called "Chemical Ali" because of his use of chemical weapons in mass killings of Iraqi Kurds], San Jawarno, whose father and other family members were killed in attacks directed by "Chemical Ali" said, "Now my father is resting in peace in his grave because Chemical Ali will be executed."

The two events, the bombing in Pakistan and the words of the bereaved son whose father was killed, are not unrelated. We must speak up, at every forum, in our homes, our churches, synagogues, mosques and temples, in our legislative bodies, wherever an opportunity exists, to convince political leaders, community leaders, religious leaders, anyone who will listen, that the death penalty has no reason to exist, promotes violence, and brings peace to no one: in the grave or not.

That was to be the end of my plea to abolish the death penalty. Then I read a report from Amnesty International about the 13-year-old girl who was stoned to death in a stadium packed with 1,000 spectators in Kismayo, Somalia. Her offense? Islamic militants accused her of adultery after she reported she had been raped by three men.

The Death Penalty Is a Random Act of Brutality

Will this senseless, inhumane killing ever end?

Perhaps. The brutality of the death penalty and of Islamic militants can end, if we speak out against it, wherever it exists, in any shape, in any form.

The death penalty is a random act of brutality. Its application throughout the United States is random, depending on where the murder occurred, the race and economic status of who committed the murder, the race and economic status of the person murdered and, of course, the quality of the legal defense.

I'm proud of the people of the state of New Jersey for electing political leaders who ended this random act of brutality. And I applaud Amnesty International for alerting the good people of the world to the brutality of the Islamic militants in Somalia who stoned to death that poor girl.

No good comes from the death penalty, whether it's imposed by duly elected governments, or by radical, religious fanatics. No good.

The burden of proof in the court of public opinion should be on those advocating for the death penalty. That burden has not been met.

Just ask Byron Halsey. Or Troy Davis. Or, if you could, that 13-year-old girl.

| "Justice truly is, as the book of God's
truth says, 'Life for life.'"

Christian Doctrine
Supports Capital Punishment

Bryan Fischer

Bryan Fischer is the host of Focal Point, *a daily talk radio program on American Family Radio, a division of the American Family Association. In the following viewpoint, Fischer argues that Christian doctrine supports capital punishment. He highlights parts of the Bible that, he contends, prove that it allows, and even advocates, killing as a punishment for murder. Capital punishment is most effective at deterring murder, he argues, when executions are performed quickly, soon after conviction. Fischer also notes that recent polls seem to indicate continuing support for the death penalty.*

As you read, consider the following questions:

1. When was capital punishment instituted by God, according to Fischer?

2. What does Fischer say would never have taken place if the United States had followed the standards for capital punishment found in Scripture?

3. According to Fischer, what percentage of Americans were found to support the death penalty in a 2010 Gallup poll?

Capital punishment was instituted by God following the flood of Noah. According to Genesis 9:5–6, God says, "From his fellow man I will require a reckoning for the life of man. Whoever sheds the blood of man, by man shall his blood be shed, for God made man in his image."

Here God is clearly delegating his authority to man—"by man shall his blood be shed"—to carry out the death penalty for the wanton taking of innocent human life. God himself is the one who is requiring this "reckoning for the life of man," because the murderer has destroyed someone created "in his image." Murder defaces and destroys the image of God, and for that God demands an accounting.

Prior to the flood, capital punishment was not allowed as a punishment for crime or as a deterrent for homicide. In fact, God himself declared that he would take vengeance "sevenfold" on anyone who punished Cain for his cold-blooded murder of Abel (Genesis 4:15).

It is as if God was saying, "Alright, you think capital punishment is barbaric. We'll do it your way . . . and see how that works out." And so mankind did, from the days of Cain until the days of Noah. How well did this kinder, gentler approach to justice work?

Vigilante Justice Prevailed Without Capital Punishment

It led to vigilante justice and barbarism, as men took matters of punishment into their own hands. Said Lamech [a patriarch in Genesis], "I have killed a man for wounding me, a young man for striking me. If Cain's revenge is sevenfold, then Lamech's is seventy-sevenfold" (Genesis 4:23–24). So vigilante justice, without God's authorization, was almost immediately exercised for non-capital offenses.

And by the time Noah arrived, the lack of a system of justice had so contributed to social deterioration and the collapse of character that "the wickedness of man was great in the earth, and . . . every intention of the thoughts of his heart was only evil continually" (Genesis 6:5). There was nothing for God to do but wipe everything out and start over. It was much like finding an 18-month-old carton of cottage cheese in the back of a refrigerator when the power's been out during the heat of summer. There's nothing to salvage. You have to dump the lot and start with a fresh container. This was the story of the flood.

So God established a new rule following the wild, wild East of the pre-flood days. From now on, God said, murder will be dealt with through capital punishment.

The Bible Contains Clearly Established Standards for Capital Punishment

This standard is reestablished in the Ten Commandments, where God succinctly commands, "You shall not murder" (Exodus 20:13).

The King James version, "Thou shalt not kill," has led some to erroneously believe that God was prohibiting killing of every kind, but he most certainly was not. The Sixth Commandment is specifically a command against cold-blooded murder. Killing in self-defense, war, and as punishment for murder are not only permitted but prescribed in the Scripture.

In fact, on the next page on the book of Exodus, in chapter 21, there are six specific crimes for which capital punishment is the prescribed penalty. As an aside, it's worth noting that the death penalty was mandated for participation in the slave trade: "Whoever steals a man and sells him, and anyone found in possession of him, shall be put to death" (Exodus 21:16).

In other words, if the United States had simply followed the standards found in Scripture, slaves never would have appeared on our shores, slavery never would have been an issue, and the Civil War would never have been fought. Then, as always, the Scriptures show us the way forward not just personally but politically as well.

Capital punishment is reaffirmed by the apostle Paul in the book of Romans as the antidote to vigilante justice and social chaos. He tells us in Romans 12:19, "Beloved, never avenge yourselves, but leave it to the wrath of God, for it is written, 'Vengeance is mine, I will repay, says the Lord.'" How does the Lord exact vengeance? As Paul immediately goes on to say, through the instrumentality of the state. Civil government has been invested with God's own authority to execute justice, including capital punishment. Government "does not bear the sword in vain," Paul says in Romans 13:4. A sword, of course, was an instrument of lethal force.

And for what purpose does civil government bear the sword? Paul immediately explains: "For he is the servant of God, and avenger who carries out God's wrath on the wrongdoer" (Romans 13:4).

It bears emphasizing that capital punishment is thus not just an Old Testament concept, but is reaffirmed as a principle of justice under the terms of the New Covenant in Christ.

Executions Deter Murderers

Solomon adds an important word of wisdom, on the subject of deterrence. Many argue—falsely it turns out—that capital punishment is no deterrent at all. Well, it certainly deters the murderer from killing anybody ever again, which sounds like deterrence to me.

But the Scripture indicates that unless capital punishment is carried out in a timely manner, it not only loses its deterrent force but actually makes things worse instead of better.

"Because the sentence against an evil deed is not executed speedily, the heart of the children of man is fully set to do evil" (Ecclesiastes 8:11).

Keeping murderers and serial killers alive on death row for a decade or more has no deterrent effect whatsoever, and yet that's what we're doing. According to the Bureau of Justice [Statistics], the average time between sentencing and execution in America is now up to 169 months, or just over 14 years. This is up from 50 months in 1977.

By the time the sentence is carried out, the public—and potential murderers who might have had some sense scared into them—have forgotten all about the crime. There is simply no connection in the public mind between crime and capital punishment.

Contrast this, for instance, with the fate of the conspirators who worked together to assassinate Abraham Lincoln. He was assassinated on April 14, 1865. The plotters had been apprehended, tried, and hung by the neck until dead by July 6, a scant 83 days later.

There Is Still Support for the Death Penalty

According to an article [by] Billy Hallowell on The Blaze, there still is a significant residue of Judeo-Christian morality left when it comes to the death penalty. Gallup found in 2010 that 64% of Americans support the death penalty while just 29% oppose it. This is an encouraging result, given the relentless brainwashing from the Left to convince us otherwise. (It's worth noting that as recently as 1995, the split was 80–16 in favor of executing murderers.)

Bizarrely, in 2004 fewer people who went to church weekly favored the death penalty (65%) compared to those who never went (71%). This is likely due to the way in which the gospel of Christ has been feminized by the modern church, all its firm edges sanded off in order not to offend. It's sobering to think that people outside the church have a more biblical view of justice than those inside the church, which certainly is an indictment of the teaching coming from America's pulpits.

Critics argue that capital punishment demonstrates a low view of the value of human life. It's exactly the reverse. It is imposing the death penalty that enables a culture to declare its highest regard for life. With the death penalty, society says that human life is so valuable that if someone takes a human life without just cause he must forfeit his own life in return. Justice truly is, as the book of God's truth says, "Life for life."

> "Some crimes are so serious and so heinous that they seem to cry out for the ultimate punishment of death. And yet the Gospel message is forever one of forgiveness, of reconciliation, of committed charity toward all without exceptions."

Christian Doctrine Does Not Support Capital Punishment

United States Conference of Catholic Bishops

The United States Conference of Catholic Bishops (USCCB) is the official organization of the Catholic hierarchy in the United States. In the following viewpoint, the USCCB states that there is a growing awareness that preventing violence by using or threatening violence is morally wrong and ineffective. Even though it may seem that death is a just punishment for particularly brutal crimes, the USCCB posits that the Gospel advocates forgiveness for all sins and transgressions. With other forms of punishment available, the USCCB argues, capital punishment is not an effective cure for society's greatest ills and crimes. Furthermore, the USCCB concludes, prisoners can change and find redemption through ministry outreach, bible study, and prayer.

"Life Matters: The Death Penalty," www.usccb.org. Reproduced by permission.

As you read, consider the following questions:

1. How many death row inmates have been exonerated by DNA testing and other conclusive forms of evidence, according to the viewpoint?

2. To what does the viewpoint state that the Fifth Commandment has always been understood to refer?

3. According to the viewpoint, what was the name of the rapist who went on to become a brother of the Order of Capuchin Franciscans?

The death penalty may make us think that we have eliminated a problem—but a person, even a criminal, is never a problem to be destroyed. It lulls us into thinking we have addressed the problem, but we have not really dealt with the deeper issues of what has gone wrong in society when violent crime is so widespread. Death is an all too simple "solution" for a much more complex set of problems we need to face as a society. There are as many degrees of guilt and culpability as there are crimes, yet the death penalty imposes one definitive, final, indiscriminate punishment on all, halting the action of the Holy Spirit on the condemned person's soul for eternity.

We know all too well the inadequacies of our society. In a real sense, our society's dysfunctions breed our criminals through poverty, fatherlessness, discrimination, injustice, lack of opportunity, and hopelessness. How much of the gang violence linked to the drug trade is occasioned by the addiction of the whole society to illegal drugs we use to escape reality? And many of our social pathologies make us more prone to crime and violence. We don't fix those problems by executing people. The death penalty just aggravates the injustices we have not yet been able to overcome.

The Death Penalty Has Serious Flaws

Despite the virtues of our justice system, we have to honestly admit it also has serious limitations. With scandalous frequency, people on death row have later been shown to be innocent of the crime for which they were convicted. DNA testing and other conclusive forms of evidence have resulted in the exoneration of well over 100 death row inmates. Nor can we overlook the fact that persons with mental illness or intellectual disabilities are put to death, despite their lesser degrees of culpability. But the death penalty once applied is irrevocable, and human life cannot be given back once eliminated.

As time goes on, our society seems increasingly reluctant to impose the death penalty, as it is imposed far less frequently now. There seems to be a growing consciousness that there is something wrong about using violence to discourage violence, that it serves no good purpose. We would be better as a people if we were to end it altogether. Many families of victims, too, are hopeful of seeing an end to the death penalty, feeling that no punishment can bring back their loved one and that it is better to forgive and hope for a change on the part of the criminal.

A Better Way

People instinctively know it is better to let the offender remain in prison and, hopefully over time, repent of his crime and change his life. To that end, the goal of Christian prison ministry was beautifully expressed by Pope Benedict XVI:

"Chaplains and their collaborators are called to be heralds of God's infinite compassion and forgiveness. . . . They are entrusted with the weighty task of helping the incarcerated rediscover a sense of purpose so that, with God's grace, they can reform their lives, be reconciled with their families and friends, and, insofar as possible, assume the responsibilities and duties which will enable them to conduct upright and honest lives" (Address to the International Commission of Catholic Prison Pastoral Care, Sept. 6, 2007).

This is the way of Christian mercy and reconciliation, and a challenge to all who call themselves Christian.

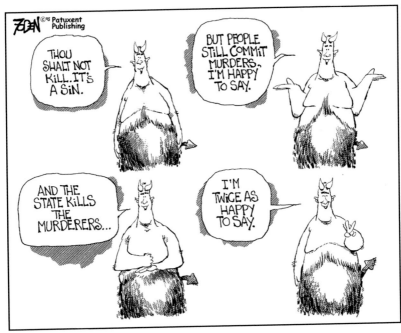

"The devil loves the death penalty," cartoon by Glenn Foden, www.CartoonStock.com. Copyright © by Glenn Foden. Reproduction rights obtainable from www.CartoonStock .com. Reproduced by permission.

We live in a culture of death: a culture torn by abortion and euthanasia, by wanton violence, war, murder, and hatred. Life is treated as if it were cheap, and many are the threats to the dignity of human life. Yet we believe that all human life is from God, and he alone is the master of life and of death. Blessed John Paul II made the defense of the dignity of all human life the centerpiece of his pontificate.

The Death Penalty Is a Complex Moral Issue

The death penalty presents itself as a complex moral issue because of the apparently conflicting demands of justice on one hand and charity on the other. Some crimes are so serious and so heinous that they seem to cry out for the ultimate punishment of death. And yet the Gospel message is forever one of forgiveness, of reconciliation, of committed charity toward all without exceptions.

Christian teaching since the time of Christ has never considered the death penalty in itself intrinsically evil. The Fifth Commandment, which instructs us *"thou shall not kill,"* has always been understood to refer to innocent human life, and not to those guilty of the most terrible crimes.

Christians have always believed in the right of *self-defense* because every person has an obligation to guard his own life as a gift from God. And society clearly has a right to defend itself from aggressors, both external (by means of war *as a last resort*) and internal (such as murderers, serial killers, terrorists, and those guilty of treason).

The question for a Christian is not so much whether there has been validity for the death penalty, but *whether it should or should not be imposed today.*

The Death Penalty Is Outmoded

And today it is clear that the death penalty no longer serves a useful purpose in protecting the sanctity of human life. Perhaps once it was the only way society could protect itself from those who would destroy the life of others, but today in most modern nations, judicial and penal systems have improved so much that they effectively remove further danger to innocent people by incarcerating the perpetrators of criminal violence. Imprisonment is effective in removing the offender from society. Importantly, it allows time for repentance and rehabilitation. And the one sure result of executing prisoners is to make us as a people more vengeful—seeking retribution and satisfying our outrage at the violent crime by more violence.

As Christians, we are asked to visit the imprisoned, minister to their needs, and encourage them to repent and change. We should never lose our conviction that even the worst offenders are our brothers and sisters in Christ, who offers forgiveness and eternal life to all. That process of reform takes time, often quite a long time. The death penalty takes that opportunity for conversion away.

Prison Can Be Transformative

One noteworthy example of a delayed conversion began with a rapist's brutal attack on an eleven-year-old girl. When she resisted him, the twenty-year-old assailant stabbed her fourteen times and left her to die. Had he not been a minor himself, he would have received the death penalty for his heinous crime. Instead, his sentence was 30 years' imprisonment. During his first three years behind bars, the murderer remained unrepentant and even hostile to a visiting priest. But after a visit from the local bishop and a dream in which his victim forgave him, he repented and resolved to lead an exemplary life. After serving his full sentence, he sought the forgiveness of his victim's family and the parish community before becoming a lay brother of the Order of Capuchin Franciscans. By now you may have guessed that his victim was St. Maria Goretti, and his name was Alessandro Serenelli. He later had the unique honor of attending the canonization of the child saint whom he had martyred. Had Alessandro been executed, the story would have had a tragically different ending.

Today, thanks to the ministry in prisons by Catholics and other Christians, countless inmates serving life sentences have allowed God to transform their lives. They lead Bible study groups, pray with fellow inmates, and counsel them to lead lives of virtue, placing all their trust in the Lord's merciful love.

Periodical and Internet Sources Bibliography

The following articles have been selected to supplement the diverse views presented in this chapter.

Roger Ebert	"Nobody Has the Right to Take Another Life," *Chicago Sun-Times*, January 4, 2012.
Liz Halloran	"Death Penalty Retains Support, Even with Pro-Life Catholics, Despite Flaws," NPR, September 23, 2011. www.npr.org.
Robert P. Jones	"Like Rick Perry, Most 'Pro-Life' Americans OK with Death Penalty," *Washington Post*, September 15, 2011.
Sarah Joseph	"Troy Davis, the Death Penalty, and International Human Rights Law," Castan Centre for Human Rights Law, September 28, 2011. http://castancentre.com.
Lawrence Nelson and Brandon Ashby	"Rethinking the Ethics of Physician Participation in Lethal Injection Execution," *Hastings Center Report*, May–June 2011.
Kate Pickert	"A Brief History of Lethal Injection," *Time*, November 10, 2009.
Joe Rojas-Burke	"Behind Execution of Gary Haugen, Controversy Swirls Around the Drugs Used and Who Administers Them," *Oregonian*, November 19, 2011.
Losang Tendrol	"A Buddhist Perspective on the Death Penalty," *Washington Post*, October 26, 2011.
Mark Tooley	"Churches Debate Troy Davis: Capital Punishment Again Faces Much Religious Opposition—and Renewed Support," *American Spectator*, October 3, 2011.

OPPOSING
VIEWPOINTS®
SERIES

CHAPTER 2

Does the Death Penalty Serve the Public Good?

Chapter Preface

One of the primary arguments for retaining the death penalty is the belief that it deters crime and helps preserve the lives of innocent, law-abiding citizens by removing the most dangerous criminals from society.

Indeed, there is some research indicating that capital punishment does have an impact on lowering crime. Based on findings in the 2003 article, "Does Capital Punishment Have a Deterrent Effect?," published in the *American Law and Economics Review*, researchers reported that data from more than three thousand counties from 1977 to 1996 showed that each execution, on average, resulted in eighteen fewer murders. While citing different statistics, other studies also have indicated a similar correlation between the death penalty and lower murder rates.

There are those, however, who say that there is little correlation between the death penalty and a lower incidence of crime. In fact, some point out that more than a few of the worst murders have occurred in the face of existing death penalty statutes. There also are those who say that the death penalty is ineffective as a deterrent to crime because it is aimed at the kind of people who are unlikely to be swayed by the threat of capital punishment—namely, those who assume that they will not be caught for committing criminal acts.

In a 2006 article in the *Ohio State Journal of Criminal Law*, Dr. Jeffrey A. Fagan of Columbia University states that many deterrence studies are flawed in their approach, claiming that each execution prevents anywhere from three to thirty-two murders depending on the research method. "There is no reliable, scientifically sound evidence that [shows that executions] can exert a deterrent effect. . . . These flaws and omissions in a body of scientific evidence render it unreliable as a basis for law or policy that generate life-and-death decisions. To accept it uncritically invites errors that have the most severe human costs."

On November 1, 2007, the United Nations General Assembly adopted a non-legally binding moratorium—a ban or prohibition—on the death penalty, saying that "the use of the death penalty undermines human dignity" and that "there is no conclusive evidence of the death penalty's deterrent value." The moratorium—an effort to advance human rights and eradicate the death penalty worldwide—also stated "that any miscarriage or failure of justice in the death penalty's implementation is irreversible and irreparable." The moratorium passed with a 104–54 vote, indicating a growing global trend toward elimination of the death penalty due to what some countries view as a violation of human rights. However, arguing that the resolution interfered with their sovereign rights, the United States, China, Iran, Syria, and Sudan voted against the measure.

Despite a growing global trend against the death penalty, capital punishment continues to remain a part of the US criminal justice system in a number of states throughout the country. As of mid-2012, thirty-three states still allowed for the death penalty. In recent years, however, a handful of states have abandoned the death penalty. In several other states, debate about whether the death penalty should be retained, reformed, or abolished continue to rage in the media and in other public forums. Regardless of the research presented on either side of the argument, the question of whether the death penalty is an effective deterrent to crime still is likely to continue as long as capital punishment remains an institution in the United States.

In the following chapter, the writers of the viewpoints explore whether the death penalty deters crime and whether there is merit to keeping capital punishment as an institution. Also included in this chapter is some discussion about whether victims' families are able to find closure through the criminal justice system and the death penalty.

> *"Recent studies ... have confirmed what we learned decades ago: Capital punishment does, in fact, save lives."*

The Death Penalty Deters Crime

David Muhlhausen

David Muhlhausen is an expert on criminal justice programs in the Heritage Foundation's Center for Data Analysis and a research fellow in empirical policy analysis. In the following viewpoint, Muhlhausen maintains that despite some vocal opposition to the death penalty, the American public still overwhelmingly supports capital punishment. Pointing to statistical data and research dating back to the 1960s, he also argues that the death penalty is an effective deterrent to murders and that it saves lives. Statistics prove, Muhlhausen concludes, that there is a direct relationship between executions and murder rates: The more executions there are, the lower the murder rate is, and the rate is even lower when executions are carried out quickly after sentencing. Muhlhausen also challenges arguments that the capital punishment system is racially biased, citing a 2006 RAND Corporation study that found no link between race and seeking the death penalty. Further, he states, studies that arrived at the opposite conclusion have been discredited.

As you read, consider the following questions:

1. According to the 2006 RAND study cited by Muhlhausen, what drives decisions to seek the death penalty?

2. What kinds of cases are less likely to have a death sentence, according to Richard Berk, as stated in the viewpoint?

3. What method of execution does Paul R. Zimmerman say is the most effective at providing deterrence, according to the viewpoint?

While opponents of capital punishment have been very vocal in their opposition, Gallup opinion polls consistently demonstrate that the American public overwhelmingly supports capital punishment. In Gallup's most recent poll, 67 percent of Americans favor the death penalty for those convicted of murder, while only 28 percent are opposed. From 2000 to the most recent poll in 2006, support for capital punishment consistently runs a 2:1 ratio in favor.

Despite strong public support for capital punishment, federal, state, and local officials must continually ensure that its implementation rigorously upholds constitutional protections, such as due process and equal protection of the law. However, the criminal process should not be abused to prevent the lawful imposition of the death penalty in appropriate capital cases.

Death Penalty Decisions Are Driven by Crime Rather than by Race

As of December 2005, there were 37 prisoners under a sentence of death in the federal system. Of these prisoners, 43.2 percent were white, while 54.1 percent were African American. The fact that African Americans are a majority of federal prisoners on death row and a minority in the overall United States population may lead some to conclude that the federal system discriminates against African Americans. However, there is little rigorous evidence that such disparities exist in the federal system.

Under a competitive grant process, the National Institute of Justice awarded the RAND Corporation a grant to determine whether racial disparities exist in the federal death penalty system. The resulting 2006 RAND study set out to determine what factors, including the defendant's race, victim's race, and crime characteristics, affect the decision to seek a death penalty case. Three independent teams of researchers were tasked with developing their own methodologies to analyze the data. Only after each team independently drew their own conclusions did they share their findings with each other.

When first looking at the raw data without controlling for case characteristics, RAND found that large race effects with the decision to seek the death penalty are more likely to occur when the defendants are white and when the victims are white. However, these disparities disappeared in each of the three studies when the heinousness of the crimes was taken into account. The RAND study concludes that the findings support the view that decisions to seek the death penalty are driven by characteristics of crimes rather than by race. RAND's findings are very compelling because three independent research teams, using the same data but different methodologies, reached the same conclusions.

While there is little evidence that the federal capital punishment system treats minorities unfairly, some may argue that the death penalty systems in certain states may be discriminatory. One such state is Maryland. In May 2001, then governor Parris Glendening instituted a moratorium on the use of capital punishment in Maryland in light of concerns that it may be unevenly applied to minorities, especially African Americans. In 2000, Governor Glendening commissioned University of Maryland professor of criminology Ray Paternoster to study the possibility of racial discrimination in the application of the death penalty in Maryland. The results of Professor Paternoster's study found that black defendants who murder white victims are substantially more likely to be charged with a capital crime and sentenced to death.

In 2003, Governor Robert L. Ehrlich wisely lifted the moratorium. His decision was justified. In 2005, a careful review of the study by professor of statistics and sociology Richard Berk of the University of California, Los Angeles and his coauthors found that the results of Professor Paternoster's study do not stand up to statistical scrutiny. According to Professor Berk's reanalysis, "For both capital charges and death sentences, race either played no role or a small role that is very difficult to specify. In short, it is very difficult to find convincing evidence for racial effects in the Maryland data and if there are any, they may not be additive." Further, race may have a small influence because "cases with a black defendant and white victim or 'other' racial combination are *less* likely to have a death sentence."

Research Supports Deterrence Theory

Federal, state, and local officials need to recognize that the death penalty saves lives. How capital punishment affects murder rates can be explained through general deterrence theory, which supposes that increasing the risk of apprehension and punishment for crime deters individuals from committing crime. Nobel laureate Gary S. Becker's seminal 1968 study of the economics of crime assumed that individuals respond to the costs and benefits of committing crime.

According to deterrence theory, criminals are no different from law-abiding people. Criminals "rationally maximize their own self-interest (utility) subject to constraints (prices, incomes) that they face in the marketplace and elsewhere." Individuals make their decisions based on the net costs and benefits of each alternative. Thus, deterrence theory provides a basis for analyzing how capital punishment should influence murder rates. Over the years, several studies have demonstrated a link between executions and decreases in murder rates. In fact, studies done in recent years, using sophisticated panel data methods, consistently demonstrate a strong link between executions and reduced murder incidents.

Early Research. The rigorous examination of the deterrent effect of capital punishment began with research in the 1970s by Isaac Ehrlich, currently a University of Buffalo distinguished professor of economics. Professor Ehrlich's research found that the death penalty had a strong deterrent effect. While his research was debated by other scholars, additional research by Professor Ehrlich reconfirmed his original findings. In addition, research by Professor Stephen K. Layson of the University of North Carolina at Greensboro strongly reconfirmed Ehrlich's previous findings.

Recent Research. Numerous studies published over the past few years, using panel data sets and sophisticated social science techniques, are demonstrating that the death penalty saves lives. Panel studies observe multiple units over several periods. The addition of multiple data collection points gives the results of capital punishment panel studies substantially more credibility than the results of studies that have only single before-and-after intervention measures. Further, the longitudinal [studied over a long period of time] nature of the panel data allows researchers to analyze the impact of the death penalty over time that cross-sectional data sets cannot address.

The Death Penalty Has a Proven Deterrent Effect

Using a panel data set of over 3,000 counties from 1977 to 1996, Professors Hashem Dezhbakhsh, Paul H. Rubin, and Joanna M. Shepherd of Emory University found that each execution, on average, results in 18 fewer murders. Using state-level panel data from 1960 to 2000, Professors Dezhbakhsh

Studies Conclude That the Death Penalty Deters Murders

A series of academic studies over the last half-dozen years . . . claim to settle a once hotly debated argument—whether the death penalty acts as a deterrent to murder. The analyses say yes. They count between three and 18 lives that would be saved by the execution of each convicted killer.

"Death Penalty Deters Murders, Studies Say,"
CBS News, February 11, 2009. www.cbsnews.com.

and Shepherd were able to compare the relationship between executions and murder incidents before, during, and after the U.S. Supreme Court's death penalty moratorium. They found that executions had a highly significant negative relationship with murder incidents. Additionally, the implementation of state moratoria is associated with the increased incidence of murders.

Separately, Professor Shepherd's analysis of monthly data from 1977 to 1999 found three important findings.

First, each execution, on average, is associated with three fewer murders. The deterred murders included both crimes of passion and murders by intimates.

Second, executions deter the murder of whites and African Americans. Each execution prevents the murder of one white person, 1.5 African Americans, and 0.5 persons of other races.

Third, shorter waits on death row are associated with increased deterrence. For each additional 2.75-year reduction in the death row wait until execution, one murder is deterred.

Professors H. Naci Mocan and R. Kaj Gittings of the University of Colorado at Denver have published two studies confirming the deterrent effect of capital punishment. The first study used state-level data from 1977 to 1997 to analyze the influence of executions, commutations, and removals from death row on the incidence of murder. For each additional execution, on average, about five murders were deterred. Alternatively, for each additional commutation, on average, five additional murders resulted. A removal from death row by either state courts or the U.S. Supreme Court is associated with an increase of one additional murder. Addressing criticism of their work, Professors Mocan and Gittings conducted additional analyses and found that their original findings provided robust support for the deterrent effect of capital punishment.

Two studies by Paul R. Zimmerman, a Federal Communications Commission economist, also support the deterrent effect of capital punishment. Using state-level data from 1978 to 1997, Zimmerman found that each additional execution, on average, results in 14 fewer murders. Zimmerman's second study, using similar data, found that executions conducted by electrocution are the most effective at providing deterrence.

Using a small state-level data set from 1995 to 1999, Professor Robert B. Ekelund of Auburn University and his colleagues analyzed the effect that executions have on single incidents of murder and multiple incidents of murder. They found that executions reduced single murder rates, while there was no effect on multiple murder rates.

Strong Evidence Demonstrates the Effectiveness of the Death Penalty

In summary, the recent studies using panel data techniques have confirmed what we learned decades ago: Capital punishment does, in fact, save lives. Each additional execution appears to deter between three and 18 murders. While opponents of capital punishment allege that it is unfairly used against African Americans, each additional execution deters the murder of 1.5 African Americans. Further moratoria, commuted sentences, and death row removals appear to increase the incidence of murder.

The strength of these findings has caused some legal scholars, originally opposed to the death penalty on moral grounds, to rethink their case. In particular, Professor Cass R. Sunstein of the University of Chicago has commented:

> If the recent evidence of deterrence is shown to be correct, then opponents of capital punishment will face an uphill struggle on moral grounds. If each execution is saving lives, the harms of capital punishment would have to be very great to justify its abolition, far greater than most critics have heretofore alleged.

Americans support capital punishment for two good reasons. First, there is little evidence to suggest that minorities are treated unfairly. Second, capital punishment produces a strong deterrent effect that saves lives.

> *"The conclusion was that criminals were clearly not deterred by the death penalty."*

The Death Penalty Isn't the Answer to Crime Woes

Jack Weil

Jack Weil is from Westdene, South Africa. In the following viewpoint, Weil argues that capital punishment and the death penalty do not prevent or deter crime. He contends that criminals in South Africa often believe their chances of going to jail are slight because of the corrupt law enforcement system. Since many believe there is a slim chance of going to jail, these criminals tend to believe the likelihood of an execution is slight as well.

As you read, consider the following questions:

1. Who is Kellow Chesney, according to the viewpoint?

2. According to Weil, public hangings could attract crowds of up to how many?

3. Who was John Gleeson, as stated in the viewpoint?

Many South Africans believe that the reintroduction of the death penalty will automatically bring down our crime rate.

Regretfully, there is little data to support the belief that a draconian legal system in itself reduces crime.

Kellow Chesney's book *The Victorian Underworld* has reference to our South African situation; the Victorians also tried to use the death penalty as a means of controlling criminal elements.

Chesney writes that Victorians lived under a harsh legal system where the death penalty was applicable to many crimes, ranging from treason to murder, attempted murder, counterfeiting, stock theft and other property offences.

The death penalty was carried out in the form of public hangings and these events could attract crowds of up to 100,000. (The 1849 hanging of a notorious criminal by the name of John Gleeson required the authorities to lay on special trains to cope with the crowds that were attracted to his execution).

Often these public hangings were clumsily managed, and a criminal could survive the initial drop at the gallows without having his neck broken.

Executioners would have to pull on the dangling body until strangulation occurred.

It was also common practice to leave the body hanging on the scaffold for an hour after execution before putting it in a coffin.

A Bristol prison chaplain of the time reported that out of 167 condemned criminals whom he had interviewed, only three had not witnessed an execution.

The conclusion was that criminals were clearly not deterred by the death penalty.

As Chesney observes, the realisation by the authorities that "criminals (were) more deterred by the probability of being caught than by a ferocious code" spurred the authorities to improve the efficiencies of the police.

These findings are applicable to our South African situation.

Potential Murderers' Perceptions of and Responses to Capital Punishment

Much of the panel research simply assumes that potential murderers respond to the objective risk of execution. There are significant complexities in computing this risk even for a well-informed researcher, let alone for a potential murderer. . . . None of the measures that are used in the research have been shown to be a better measure of the risk of execution than any others. . . .

The committee [Committee on Deterrence and the Death Penalty, National Research Council] is also skeptical that potential murderers can possibly estimate the objective risk, whatever it is. Hence, there is good reason to believe that perceived risk deviates from the objective risk. The research does not address how potential murderers' perceptions of capital punishment—and, more generally, noncapital sanction risks—are formed. . . .

There is no basis for assuming that the trend line specified by researchers corresponds to the trend line (if any) that is perceived by potential murderers. If researchers and potential murderers do not perceive trends the same way, then time-series analyses do not correctly identify what potential murderers perceive as deviations. Because of this basic flaw in the research, the committee has no basis for assessing whether the findings of time-series studies reflect a real effect of executions on homicides or are artifacts of models that incorrectly specify how deviations from a trend line cause potential murderers to update their forecasts of the future course of executions.

Daniel S. Nagin and John V. Pepper, eds.,
Deterrence and the Death Penalty.
Washington, DC: The National Academies Press, 2012.

Our inefficient/corrupt police service and courts, which produce a low conviction rate, will be the same people tasked with implementing the death penalty.

Criminals, who believe that their chances of going to jail are slight, will in all probability also assume that their chances of being executed are equally slight.

Their attitude that crime pays will in no way be altered.

Threatening criminals with death is not a deterrent if you are largely unable to carry out that threat.

There are no short cuts. The only way to reduce our crime rate is to improve the efficiencies of our police services and our courts.

Simply put, a high rate of apprehension by the police and conviction by the courts will result in decreased criminal behaviour.

> "One need not put aside a philosophical belief about capital punishment to recognize the financial impracticality of the system."

The Cost of the Death Penalty Outweighs Its Benefits to Society

Julie Delcour

Julie Delcour is an associate at Tulsa World *in Oklahoma. In the following viewpoint, Delcour argues that the death penalty is the most expensive, financially impractical punishment for convicted murderers. People may be divided on the morality of capital punishment and whether it is an effective deterrent to crime, but Delcour points out that no one can dispute the high cost of the death penalty. As Delcour argues, the cost of one execution is significantly higher than life imprisonment without parole. At a time when state budgets are slim and cutbacks are the norm, Delcour maintains that the high cost of the death penalty system makes little sense—especially when so many law enforcement officials consider it an ineffective deterrent against homicides and the least efficient use of taxpayer dollars.*

As you read, consider the following questions:

1. What does Delcour say is the average cost of one death penalty case in Oklahoma, from arrest to execution?

2. What were the findings of the 2008 poll of police chiefs, as stated in the viewpoint?

3. When did New Mexico abolish its death penalty, according to Delcour?

"I no longer believe you can fix the death penalty. (It) throws millions of dollars down the drain. Give a law enforcement professional like me that $250 million, and I'll show you how to reduce crime. The death penalty isn't anywhere on my list."

—*New Jersey police chief James Abbott*

Those Jersey boys know how to lay it on the line. Abbott made that observation years ago when asked his opinion of whether his state should scrap its costly death penalty law. New Jersey did so in 2007.

Forget all the arguments about the rightness or wrongness of capital punishment—if it is a powerful deterrent or morally repugnant, if its use is appropriate for worst-of-the-worst crimes.

Should death penalty laws eventually go by the wayside here and elsewhere, their demise won't be based on philosophical debates.

The issue will come down to the bottom line. In this era of fiscal peril, legislatures and voters must decide: Do they continue sustaining the nation's most expensive punishment option—for a relatively small number of convicted murders—when other needs, including education, health care, infrastructure and public safety, go wanting?

Budget cutbacks in Oklahoma since 2008 have resulted in layoffs and the drastic slashing of services and programs.

The state's safety net, which so many people rely upon, is ripping at the seams.

Prisons are at capacity, yet the per capita violent crime rate remains among the highest in the U.S.

No reliable figures exist for how much Oklahoma's death penalty system costs. Suffice it to say it's tens of millions of dollars.

Throwing political caution to the wind, some leaders have suggested dropping the death penalty. State Sen. Constance Johnson, D-Oklahoma City, was roundly ignored when she proposed scrapping that system and going to a far less costly life-without-parole system.

A few states have abolished their systems in light of cost. In the 34 states with a death penalty [in 2011], some are asking: Can the needs of so many be sacrificed to pay for punishment of so few?

Death Penalty Cases Cost Millions

Nationally, about 3,200 people are on state and federal death rows, including 69 in Oklahoma. The average cost, from arrest to execution, for a single death penalty case ranges from $1 million to $3 million. Those costs, on a per offender basis, rank as among the most expensive part of criminal justice systems. That fact has prompted countless studies, including an eye-popping one released in June in California.

That state has the nation's largest and costliest death row—714 inmates. Since reinstating its death penalty in 1978, California has conducted nearly 2,000 capital trials and has executed 13 people. Over those 33 years, the death penalty system cost the state $4.6 billion.

Divided up, that equates to $308 million per execution.

For a state teetering on the brink of financial collapse, here's how the $4.6 billion broke down: pretrial/trial costs, $1.94 billion; automatic appeals and state habeas corpus peti-

The High Cost of Executions Is Paid by Local Governments

The costs of administering capital punishment are prohibitive. Even in states where prosecutors infrequently seek the death penalty, the price of obtaining convictions and executions ranges from $2.5 million to $5 million per case . . . , compared to less than $1 million for each killer sentenced to life without parole. . . .

The burden of these costs is borne by local governments, often diverting precious resources not only from police, but also from health care, infrastructure, and education, or forcing counties to borrow money or raise taxes.

Jeffrey A. Fagan,
"Capital Punishment: Deterrent Effects &
Capital Costs," 2010. www.law.columbia.edu.

tions, $0.925 billion; federal habeas petitions, $0.775 billion; costs of incarceration, $1 billion.

In light of those costs, backers of a stalled legislative bill to abolish the death penalty recently kicked off a campaign to put the question on the November 2012 ballot.

If approved, California's death penalty laws would become history. The measure would do something else, which could persuade voters to pass it: $100 million from the state's general fund—the estimated savings from eliminating death row—would be distributed over the next four fiscal years to local police for solving more homicides and rapes.

A North Carolina study also performed a cost-benefit analysis and found a $2 million difference between a death sentence and a life-without-parole sentence. In Texas, a death penalty case costs about $3 million, three times the cost of imprisoning an inmate for 40 years.

In Maryland, a death penalty case costs about three times more than a case in which the prosecutor does not seek the death penalty, according to an Urban Institute study. Since 2000, death sentences across the U.S. have dropped precipitously.

Law Enforcement Officials Say the Death Penalty Is Ineffective

A 2008 poll of police chiefs, often cited by Richard [C.] Dieter, executive director of the Death Penalty Information Center in Washington, D.C., produced surprising answers. Almost all the chiefs surveyed ranked the death penalty last among their priorities for crime fighting, saying that they did not believe—based on murder rates—that it deterred homicides. Most rated it as the least efficient use of limited taxpayer dollars.

New York abolished its death penalty in 2007. In the many years the law was on the books, no death sentences were upheld by its courts nor was any offender executed.

New Mexico abolished its death penalty in 2009.

The death penalty is widely favored in Oklahoma, which has the executions to prove it. For many, keeping it as an option is crucial—whatever the cost. But is that an informed stance?

One need not put aside a philosophical belief about capital punishment to recognize the financial impracticality of the system.

Oklahoma leaders should undertake a study to determine the cost of the death penalty system here. Relying on those results, Oklahomans could make a more informed choice about whether to keep it. Ultimately, the question comes down to priorities.

"The real issue is the more fundamental debate about whether a sentence of death is ever an appropriate penalty for the state to impose upon a person convicted of the most serious forms of murder. That debate rests on philosophical and moral views about justice, not on dollars and cents."

The Death Penalty Is Essential, and Its Cost Is Irrelevant

Derek Schmidt

Derek Schmidt is a former Republican state senator and current attorney general for the state of Kansas. In the following viewpoint, Schmidt argues that the death penalty is still needed despite opponents' argument that capital punishment should be abolished due to excessive cost. The real issue, Schmidt argues, is not about cost. Instead, the fundamental issue has to do with philosophical views about justice and whether the death penalty is an appropriate punishment for those convicted of particularly horrific cases of murder. The viewpoint touches on a proposed

Derek Schmidt, "A Case for Retaining the Kansas Death Penalty," *The Kansas Prosecutor*, Fall 2009, pp. 7–8. Copyright © 2009 by The Kansas Prosecutor. All rights reserved. Reproduced by permission.

piece of legislation designed to abolish the death penalty in Kansas, and Schmidt argues that the current, well-designed death penalty law is still needed and should remain in effect.

As you read, consider the following questions:

1. According to Schmidt, on what are key cost factors in the Legislative Division of Post Audit's final report based?

2. Why does Schmidt say no one has been executed in Kansas within the fifteen years following the reinstatement of the death penalty?

3. What is a possible sentence for sex predators who prey on children, according to Jessica's Law?

For as long as the death penalty has been reinstated in Kansas, there have been efforts in the legislature to abolish it.

The most recent strategy to abolish capital punishment in Kansas emerged in 2004, when a penalty of life in prison without the possibility of parole was enacted into law as an alternative to the death penalty in capital murder cases. This new sentencing option won broad support in the legislature from both supporters and opponents of the death penalty because it was presented as an additional sentencing alternative that would be available on a case-by-case basis to prosecutors, judges, and jurors in capital cases as they work to do justice in the case before them.

Opponents of the death penalty then commissioned the Legislative Division of Post Audit to conduct a study of the financial cost of carrying out a death sentence as opposed to a sentence of life without parole in capital cases. Despite warnings from the Post Audit staff that the subject really did not lend itself to accurate quantitative comparison, the study was ordered and was conducted to the best of the auditors' ability. The final report makes clear that key cost figures in the report are based on assumptions and not on data, but nonetheless the mere existence of this report is now often cited by death penalty opponents as evidence of an excessive financial cost of capital punishment.

The Economic Recession Sparks Concerns About the Death Penalty's Costs

Then came the current economic recession. Dramatic state budget shortfalls created an environment in which every penny of state spending became subject to strict legislative scrutiny. In this atmosphere, opponents of the death penalty advanced this argument for which they had spent years laying the foundation: The state should abolish the death penalty because it costs less to impose a sentence of life without the possibility of parole.

The result was introduced during the 2009 legislative session of Senate Bill 208. That legislation was presented as an effort to prospectively abolish the death penalty while leaving intact the death sentences of murderers already under sentence of death in Kansas. The bill received hearings in the Senate Judiciary Committee, and when time came for the committee to vote, the measure initially was defeated. A day later, however, the committee reconsidered, one vote changed, and the bill was narrowly reported to the full Senate.

During debate in the full Senate, I pointed out numerous shortcomings in the drafting of the bill. It became clear to supporters and opponents alike that the legislation, if enacted, was likely to have serious unintended consequences. As a result, the Senate sent the bill back to the Judiciary Committee without bringing it to a final vote. The measure has now been committed to study in the Judicial Council, which is attempting to resolve the many technical problems with the bill.

So that's the status of the debate. It's clear the issue will be back, probably during the 2010 legislative session, so interested parties on all sides of the debate should prepare to engage. I have a few observations on the situation:

- The real issue is not cost. As it always has been and always will be: The real issue is the more fundamental debate about whether a sentence of death is ever an appropriate penalty for the state to impose upon a person convicted of the most serious forms of murder. That debate rests on philosophical and moral views about justice, not on dollars and cents.

- The vote count in the Senate likely is close. This is an issue that does not, and in my view should not, follow partisan or ideological lines. There are senators across the political spectrum who support capital punishment, and there are senators across the spectrum who oppose it. I make this point to underscore the reality that every single senator's vote counts on this, and people with strong feelings on either side of the debate would be wise to engage with their local legislators early and thoughtfully.

- This coming session is the time for both sides to mobilize. During consideration of the proposed repeal in 2009, death penalty opponents were organized and engaged. They testified in the Judiciary Committee and made their case. People who support keeping the death penalty on the books were less organized and did not initially engage the committee. They need to be on notice this year: 2010 is the time to engage and make the case for keeping the law intact.

Current Death Penalty Law Is Necessary

A narrowly crafted, sparingly used death penalty with adequate procedural safeguards to protect against injustice should remain on the books in Kansas. Our current law fits that description. There are homicides so serious, so heinous, that justice requires a jury of the defendant's peers to have the option of imposing a sentence of death as a consequence of the defendant's terrible crime. Not every victim's family will want that option imposed, but some will. The option should remain available to prosecutors, judges, and juries.

Many of the criticisms of capital punishment leveled in other states do not apply in Kansas because of the narrow scope of our state's capital murder statute and the sparing application of the death penalty by prosecutors. The number of defendants under sentence of death in our state is small. Fifteen years after reinstatement of the death penalty, no execution has yet been carried out because of the thorough nature of appellate review to ensure no innocent person is executed. No serious claim of actual innocence has become a focus of the post-conviction legal strategy of a defendant under sentence of death.

When the Judicial Council completes its review of Senate Bill 208, the bill will be substantially better constructed than it was previously. But significant issues will remain even within the text of the bill because some of the drafting questions are intertwined with basic policy choices that are beyond the scope of the Judicial Council's work. At least two major areas of concern will remain.

First, it may not be possible to prospectively repeal the death penalty statute while leaving intact and eventually carrying out the death sentences of those defendants already sentenced. Any change in the law inevitably will give rise to more legal challenges by those already under sentence of death, and the appellate history to date suggests that the Kansas Supreme Court tends to look sympathetically on claims that the death penalty statute is defective. It also is not difficult to imagine that, if the death penalty were abolished prospectively, the same arguments that led the political branches of government to adopt a prospective repeal would, over years as appeals drag on, be brought to bear on the individual cases that were purported to have been grandfathered. All three branches of state government would feel the pressure to apply the reasoning of those arguments to the small and finite number of persons under sentence of death, and all three branches have within their power the ability to prevent the carrying out of those already-imposed death sentences. The effect of any repeal on currently sentenced defendants is, at best, an unpredictable roll of the dice.

Second, this debate also raises serious policy questions about the definition of "life without the possibility of parole" and under what circumstances it should be imposed. On the back end of the process, for example, it remains to be settled whether the governor should retain the power to pardon or commute the sentence of a defendant sentenced to life without the possibility of parole. On the front end of the process, there should be consideration of whether the list of aggravating circumstances that can lead to a life-without-parole sentence should be broadened to include more homicides than the narrow universe covered by the capital murder statute. It also should be considered whether other serious person felonies, such as certain rapes, should be considered for life-without-parole sentences, just as the legislature in the 2006 Jessica's Law made life without parole a possible sentence for certain sex predators who prey on children.

In the end, this ongoing debate will once again boil itself down to the fundamental policy question that always has been at the core of the death penalty debate in Kansas: Should ordering a state-sponsored execution of a murderer ever be an option available to a jury of the defendant's peers in rendering justice in the case before it?

In my view of justice, I believe the answer to that basic question remains "yes."

> "Do we think that telling our story will change anyone's mind on the death penalty? Probably not, but we do hope it makes you think. . . . Do we agree with the death penalty? In this case . . . you bet we do."

Death Penalty Would End Punishment of Victim's Family

Irl Stambaugh and Gary Stambaugh

Irl Stambaugh is a retired police officer, and Gary Stambaugh worked as sergeant at arms for the Alaska state senate. In the following viewpoint, the Stambaugh brothers argue for the death penalty based on their experience following the murder of their sister, Jody, in Fairbanks, Alaska. Living in a state that has never had a death penalty, the authors explain, has meant that the Stambaugh family has had to sit through multiple parole hearing requests since Jody Stambaugh's murder on December 10, 1972. The Stambaugh brothers describe the heartache, fear, and repeated traumatization the family has had to endure every time their sister's murderer has requested a parole hearing. If their sister's murderer had been sentenced to death, they conclude, his other victims and victims' survivors would have been spared decades of suffering.

As you read, consider the following questions:

1. According to Irl and Gary Stambaugh, what did their sister's murderer, Allen Walunga, do while attending school at Mount Edgecumbe?

2. What did the parole board say in 1998 regarding Allen Walunga, according to the authors?

3. According to the authors, what did Allen Walunga say might prevent him from doing well on probation?

Our sister Jody Stambaugh was an 18-year-old University of Alaska Fairbanks student when she was raped and murdered in her dorm room during the early evening hours on Dec. 10, 1972. Her roommate was also seriously assaulted and might have been killed had not others heard the assault and come to her aid.

This horrendous crime occurred so many years ago. How could it possibly be relevant in today's discussion on the death penalty?

We should start at the beginning.

Jody, a third generation Alaskan, was raised with her two brothers in Ketchikan and Juneau. Jody was an exceptional person, always calm, always kind, and always considerate of others. After graduation from high school in Juneau, she decided to attend the University of Alaska Fairbanks.

A Known Offender

Allen Walunga spent his early years in a small community in Interior Alaska. At an early age, he became a violent sexual predator and sexually assaulted several underage girls. (He later admitted to sexually assaulting several young boys in the community during this same time period.)

So, what did the powers to be do? They shipped him off to school at Mount Edgecumbe in Sitka, Alaska.

While attending school at Mount Edgecumbe, he obtained a gas soaked rag and held it to the mouth and nose of an intoxicated female student until she went limp. He thought he had killed her so he ran away. After that incident, he moved to Fairbanks and attended high school.

During his time in Fairbanks, he was charged with pedophilia and child molestation. He was placed on probation.

He then went to the University of Alaska Fairbanks where no one inquired as to his background before they placed him in a co-ed dorm. (Juvenile records are confidential even when it involves a violent sexual predator being in contact with an entire campus of potential victims.)

The Nightmare Starts

On December 10, 1972, our lives were changed forever. Jody was murdered, another wonderful young lady was assaulted, and Walunga was taken into custody.

Then the nightmare started.

Walunga was found guilty of murder in the 1st degree and assault with the intent to kill.

Judge Van Hoomissen found that Walunga "was an extremely dangerous offender who presented a clear and present danger of killing another person if ever released from prison."

The probation officer stated in part:

If we had a death penalty in this state, I would recommend whatever that death penalty might be. This is a heinous crime and I agree that the chances for rehabilitation are poor.

A Life Sentence for Homicide Survivors

The trauma may not end once the convicted murderer is sentenced; survivors are often surprised to learn that the criminal sentences imposed and ordered are frequently *not* the sentences served. Ongoing appeals and parole hearings may easily trigger later stress reactions for the surviving family members, friends and loved ones of the victim. . . .

The combination of grief reactions and increased vulnerability to post-traumatic stress disorder often results in . . . "a life sentence" for the rest of the family after a loved one is murdered.

"Homicide Survivors,"
National Center for Victims of Crime, 2011.
www.ncvc.org.

Judge Van Hoomissen said, "This is probably the most vicious crime that I have had contact with."

He imposed a life sentence on the murder with a concurrent 15 years on the assault with intent to kill count.

At that time, our family felt that justice had been done and Walunga would remain in jail for the remainder of his life. We continued with our lives and through time minimized our grief. Our father had a serious heart attack that I will always partially attribute to the grief and sorrow he lived with after our sister's death.

The First Parole Request

Then in September of 1987 we were shocked to find out that Walunga was able to ask for a parole hearing.

So here we went again. The entire senseless murderous incident was being rehashed in a hearing. As a family, as individuals, and as victims, we responded to Walunga's request, and he was denied.

In 1989 he requested commutation of his sentence and was denied.

In 1991 he tested the waters and applied for a parole hearing.

In 1992 he applied for a parole hearing and was denied.

In 1997 he tested the waters and applied for a parole hearing.

In 1998 he applied for a parole hearing and was denied. The parole board said that the release of the defendant on discretionary parole was wholly out of the question and that the board would never again consider another parole application.

The family and victims breathed another sigh of relief that it was finally over, and Walunga would remain in jail.

We Thought It Was Over

Then unknown to any family member or victim, the new parole board in 2005 decided that it would consider discretionary parole applications every 10 years, despite what any prior board had decided and contrary to what Judge Van Hoomissen recommended in his sentencing report.

In 2008 Walunga got a parole hearing. It is interesting to note Walunga was being represented by a high-profile Anchorage attorney. Walunga entered into the record a psychiatric report he had paid for. We were not entitled to see it because we were told that it was a medical record.

Sorry?

In addition, Walunga provided the board and victims with a report that says in part he is sorry for the murder (however, he fails to mention that there was a second victim). He says he has found God. He thinks he will do well on probation unless he is confronted with "his temptation to form adulterous friendships with abnormally large breasted women." He also fails to mention his previous sexual misconduct.

This is not an attempt to bash the probation/parole department at corrections. Through it all, after having to deal with antiquated rules, regulations and statutes, they have done a remarkable job in keeping Walunga behind bars where he cannot harm anyone in our communities.

After another emotionally grueling hearing for us, Walunga's request was again denied.

37 Years of Heartache

If you can, imagine the heartache we have endured over the last 37 years, always fearing that this may be the hearing where he gets his way. During that same time period, life continues on. Our father and mother have passed away, and our children have grown but we continue to attend hearings. As we promised our mother, we will continue to attend hearings.

The other victim has raised a family, but continues to attend hearings fearing that Walunga will be released.

Do we think that telling our story will change anyone's mind on the death penalty? Probably not, but we do hope it makes you think.

Do we think my sister would agree with the death penalty? Probably not. She was a better person than a lot of us.

Do we agree with the death penalty? In this case with the above set of facts, you bet we do.

> *"We need to ask how victims might feel when others suggest that any kind of permanent 'leaving it behind' is possible. Is it truly helpful to victims' families to be made promises like that?"*

The Death Penalty Does Not Fulfill Survivors' Needs for Closure

Susan Bandes, as told to Murder Victims' Families for Human Rights

Susan Bandes is a law professor who has taught at Florida State University and DePaul University College of Law. In the following viewpoint, an interview between Bandes and Murder Victims' Families for Human Rights, Bandes discusses the common arguments for using the death penalty as a way for victims' families to find closure. Bandes points out that some victims may not experience closure after a murderer is put to death but instead may find closure through other means. According to Bandes, prosecutors seeking a death sentence often argue for the death penalty under the pretext of providing closure for the victims' families. But Bandes says that there is a valid question about whether true closure can be found in the criminal justice system. She argues that there is no cure-all for the suffering endured by survivors of homicide and that arguments that the death penalty offers closure for them does not reflect their individual realities.

As you read, consider the following questions:

1. When does Bandes say the terms "closure" and "the death penalty" were first mentioned together?

2. According to Bandes, what are some of the ways that people find closure following the murder of a loved one?

3. What does Bandes say has given people "permission" to support the death penalty?

*[M*urder Victims' Families for Human Rights:] In your recent article, "Victims, 'Closure,' and the Sociology of Emotion," you point out that the emphasis on "closure" is actually a fairly recent phenomenon.*

[Susan Bandes:] Yes, the whole idea of closure is relatively new, and the link between closure and the death penalty is particularly new. If you ran a search for the terms "closure" and "the death penalty," you'd find that the terms were not mentioned together until 1989. But just twelve years later in 2001, a national poll asked whether the death penalty is fair because it gives closure to the families of murder victims. Sixty percent of the respondents agreed with that statement.

How do you think those respondents came to believe that idea?

People had by then been repeatedly told, through the media, that the death penalty offers closure to victims' families, so then they gave that answer when asked by the media. It's a feedback loop that we see all the time.

Part of the problem is that we think we're having a national conversation about the death penalty, but in large part we're really just answering pollsters' questions. We're not given free rein to express our deepest thoughts, our most complex thoughts. So it's hard to know what people mean when they give a yes or no answer, because they weren't asked to explain. We can only guess.

I do think there's also something about the idea of closure that really seized people's imaginations. It rang a bell: Of course victims must need closure, must need to move on. The idea seems to touch something deep in people, something that they want to believe.

Defining Closure Is Individual

What does closure actually mean?

The claim of my recent article is that we really don't know what we're talking about when we use the term closure. On a societal level, we need to be clearer about what we might mean, and then even if we do succeed at defining closure, we have to ask whether the legal system is the right place to get it.

The most common assumption is that giving closure means giving people a sense of finality or a sense that they have been heard, that their loss has been respected. That probably does have roots in what people truly need, but what gets problematic is the next part: "so that then they can leave the problem behind." We need to ask how victims might feel when others suggest that any kind of permanent "leaving it behind" is possible. Is it truly helpful to victims' families to be made promises like that?

For some victims, closure might mean getting answers to questions that they have, whether by actually speaking with the defendant or by trying to understand, in some other way, how someone could do a thing like this. For some victims, seeing or hearing that the person has come to take responsibility or feel remorse might be very helpful.

Closure May Not Come from the Legal System

You said a moment ago that even if we could come to a common agreement about what closure means psychologically, we need to ask whether the criminal justice system is the best place to seek it.

Prosecutors have fought victims' rights when those rights might dilute their own discretion. Part of me thinks that arguing for "closure" is a way for prosecutors to seem to be advocating for victims but actually to be advocating for death sentences. It's a very good argument to put forth when seeking a death sentence: "You, the jury, need to do this for the victim's family; you need to show how much society values this victim and you do that by imposing a death sentence."

A problem, of course, has been that victims are not monolithic. They need different things, and at different times. When victims don't want to sign on to the prosecutor's agenda, the prosecutor in many cases silences them. In the prosecution of Timothy McVeigh [an American domestic terrorist who used a bomb to destroy a federal building in Oklahoma City, killing 168 people], for example, Marilyn Knight had lost her daughter in the bombing and she did not believe in the death penalty, and the prosecutor would not allow her to give a victim impact statement.

Can the criminal justice system have therapeutic goals? Is that even a good way to think about it?

It's a good question, one that I think the current system is rather confused about. I believe that by discussing anything that happens in the courtroom as though it is therapeutic, we're having a dangerously misleading discussion. The courtroom's goal is not primarily to be a safe and therapeutic place for the people who speak there. But if we determine that the courtroom ought to be a therapeutic place, we need to think more seriously about how to make it one. For example, if we're concerned with the well-being of people within the criminal justice system, how about training judges in how to treat and react to people who are opening themselves up, giving incredibly painful testimony in a very emotionally unsafe place?

There Are Few Options for Victims or Jurors

Maybe part of the problem is that there is such a poverty of other alternatives: Where else can victims' family members get their loss publicly recognized and addressed?

Yes, I think we have seen in victims' accounts of why they chose to deliver a victim impact statement that there is a real desire to remember and honor the victim in a ritualized way, in a venerated public venue, and to have the sense that people in positions of authority, in respected public institutions, recognize and care about the loss. That might be one of the things that people mean by closure. So, what if there were other opportunities for this besides courtroom testimony? How else might a society offer this to victims?

And then, thinking along these same lines, there are also not many options available to the jury. In your article you say, "A capital jury faced with pain and grief, overcome with anger, does not have many social options at its disposal. If it wishes to take action on its empathy toward the survivor, its grief at the loss of the victim and its anger toward the defendant, its only apparent option is to vote for a sentence of death."

Yes. In effect, we have said to the jury, "We expect some kind of help from you with healing the victims' pain. You're not just here to decide the appropriate sentence based on the circumstances of the crime; you're here to deal with this pain, *but* you're deprived of most of the tools that we usually have for dealing with pain."

What if we said, instead, "You the jury have to do this and only this specific legal task; we have other arenas, other ways, of helping victims' families?"

Right. That would be something very different. If you are on a jury and you don't think it's a case in which the death penalty should be imposed, but you have been told that the death penalty is what we owe to the victim and this is what we do for victims who are valued, you're in a terrible dilemma.

Meanwhile, it's also important to remember that we don't execute everyone who has committed a murder; we don't even charge everyone capitally. So if the death penalty promises closure, this is a promise we cannot keep and are not keeping for everyone.

Victims' Needs Are Far More Complex than Closure

Taking it out of the courtroom, can you speak a bit about how the idea of closure has changed the debate publicly, politically?

In the Supreme Court's recent lethal injection decision, Justice [John Paul] Stevens said we're never going to know whether the death penalty deters future murderers; the evidence is inconclusive. That has been one major argument for the death penalty; without it, we're left with retribution. But some people are uncomfortable with retribution; maybe it sounds too much like revenge, and we don't want to be the kinds of people who take revenge. So now an idea has been introduced that is somewhat different: the idea that by supporting the death penalty, you're helping the victims attain closure. I think this has given people permission to support the death penalty—but based, again, on an idea that has no empirical grounding.

How might we challenge all this and give people a better and more in-depth understanding of these issues?

I fear that people don't like complexity and don't want to hear that there's no way to make it all better when someone has suffered a terrible loss. I think that what the members of your organization are doing is absolutely crucial: saying we've been through this experience and the idea of closure, as it's generally being used, does not match how many of us feel, making it clear that victims are complex, and victims' needs are complex.

Periodical and Internet Sources Bibliography

The following articles have been selected to supplement the diverse views presented in this chapter.

James Devitt	"Death Penalty May Not Impact Murder Rate," Futurity, February 24, 2012. www.futurity.org.
Richard C. Dieter	"Smart on Crime: Reconsidering the Death Penalty in a Time of Economic Crisis," Death Penalty Information Center, October 2009. www.deathpenaltyinfo.org.
Paul Heroux	"The Death Penalty: Questionable Evidence for Deterrence," *Huffington Post*, November 4, 2011. www.huffingtonpost.com.
Maura Kelly	"Capital Punishment: An Offence Against Victims' Relatives," *Guardian*, April 7, 2011.
Eliott C. McLaughlin	"Death Penalty's Unlikely Opponents," CNN, October 24, 2011. www.cnn.com.
New York Times	"High Cost of Death Row," September 27, 2009.
James M. Reams and Charles T. Putnam	"Making the Case for the Deterrence Effect of Capital Punishment," *New Hampshire Bar Journal*, Summer 2011.
Statesman (Austin, TX)	"Add Cost of Drugs to Death Penalty Debate," February 26, 2012.
Nathan Thornburgh	"Troy Davis' Execution: Outrage for Opponents, but Closure for Victim's Family?," *Time*, September 21, 2011.
Eric Zorn	"Can the Death Penalty Incite Murder?," *Chicago Tribune*, April 27, 2011.

**OPPOSING
VIEWPOINTS®
SERIES**

CHAPTER 3

Is the Death Penalty Applied Fairly?

Chapter Preface

The question of whether the US criminal justice system is capable of administering justice fairly and without bias continues to fuel heated debate about capital punishment throughout the country.

Some argue that despite reforms and changes over the past several decades, the death penalty system remains flawed. Opponents argue that administration of the death penalty often is unfair, racially biased, and arbitrary. Others concede that while there still appears to be some racial bias and arbitrariness in the system, progress has been made with improvements to the system. Adding to the chorus of those who raise questions about fairness are those who argue that the death penalty constitutes cruel and unusual punishment for those who are severely mentally ill or mentally impaired. In fact, some argue that individuals with severe mental illness should be exempt from the death penalty altogether.

For many, the question of fairness necessarily leads to a discussion about the reliability of evidence that is used while prosecuting criminal cases. And in recent years, DNA testing has increasingly entered the debate about fairness as it relates to the death penalty. With advances in technology, it now is possible to establish the presence of an individual at the scene of the crime. As a result, some argue that DNA testing helps ensure the just and fair implementation of the death penalty. Court rulings in recent years indicate that the use of DNA testing may continue to increase in capital punishment cases. The question that DNA testing attempts to answer is: Have we convicted the right person, or is the person we have convicted actually innocent of the crime?

In March 2011, the US Supreme Court issued a six to three ruling in *Skinner v. Switzer*, granting prisoners the right to file post-conviction civil suits to seek access to DNA evidence, which was not tested at the time of trial. While some say such evidence can lead to death row exonerations, others point out that it also can prove the guilt of the accused.

Since his conviction in 1995, Henry Skinner has maintained his innocence in the face of charges that he killed his girlfriend and her two sons. Skinner came within forty-five minutes of being executed before the US Supreme Court took up his case in 2010. Despite the ruling, there is no guarantee that Skinner will ever gain access to all of the DNA evidence that was recovered at the crime scene. As of mid-2012, Skinner was still sitting on death row in Texas.

While some say DNA testing will help resolve some issues within the death penalty system, others aren't as optimistic. Richard C. Dieter, executive director of the Death Penalty Information Center, wrote in the 2004 "Innocence and the Crisis in the American Death Penalty" report: "The era of DNA testing has not ushered in a fool-proof criminal justice system. It is not true that the problems of wrongful convictions are in the past and will not happen anymore because technology can now precisely determine guilt. Nor is it true that the death penalty can proceed unchecked under the assumption that all the inmates on death row have had ample opportunity for DNA testing."

Dieter added that in a majority of cases, attorneys and courts had to rely on other forms of evidence—like a confession by the actual killer—during criminal trials. In conclusion, Dieter said that DNA testing does not resolve inherent problems in the system. "A rarely applied and highly selective death penalty might still be subject to the arbitrariness, bias, and human fallibility that have always plagued this punishment. But the current system serves no one well. It is a system in which nearly every murder is eligible for the death penalty, and, as a result, an overwhelmed system does most cases poorly rather than a few cases reliably."

The authors of the viewpoints in the following chapter explore whether the death penalty can be applied fairly in the US criminal justice system. As part of the discussion, commentators raise questions about DNA testing, racial bias, and whether some populations—like the severely mentally ill—should be exempt from the death penalty.

"*Capital punishment has national and international implications, yet in the US . . . local officials enjoy broad powers to prosecute and execute based on groundless assumptions and bias about race.*"

The Capital Punishment System Is Still Racially Biased

David A. Love

David A. Love is a writer and the executive director of Witness to Innocence, an organization in Philadelphia, Pennsylvania, that is made up of former death row prisoners and their families. According to Love, the application of the death penalty in the United States does not appear to be based solely on the facts of a case. Rather, he says, the administration of the death penalty appears to rest more on arbitrary, unfair, and racially biased factors. African American and Hispanic inmates, Love asserts, particularly those who were found guilty of murdering a white victim, make up a vastly disproportionate percentage of death row inmates. The percentage is highest in the South, where Love contends that a history of racism is still present in the legal system.

As you read, consider the following questions:

1. According to the viewpoint, how much more likely were defendants whose victims were white to receive the death penalty?

2. What state does Love say ranked twenty-third in population and second in executions in 2011?

3. In death penalty states, who decides whether to seek the death penalty in individual cases, according to the viewpoint?

The application of the US death penalty is unfair, arbitrary and racially biased. Whether a defendant receives a death sentence depends not on the merits of the case, so much as on his or her skin colour—and the race of the victim—and the county in which the murder case was prosecuted. Two recent news items in the US provide some illustrative context.

First, the issue of bias: The North Carolina Senate recently approved Senate Bill 9 [SB9], a measure that would repeal the state's Racial Justice Act. The act, signed into law by Governor Bev Perdue in 2009, allows inmates to challenge their death sentences through statistical evidence of racial bias, including the exclusion of blacks from juries. Republican lawmakers and prosecutors opposed the law.

Fortunately, the governor vetoed SB9, which would have required prosecutors to openly confess to racism. This would have made it far more difficult for prisoners to prove racial discrimination in their sentence, despite evidence such as a study of North Carolina which found that defendants whose victims were white were 3.5 times more likely to receive a death sentence.

Second, the geographical anomalies: An analysis by the *Houston Chronicle* found that 12 of the last 13 people condemned to death in Harris County, Texas, were black. After Texas itself, Harris County is the national leader in its number

"Deadly dosage," cartoon by John Cole, www.PoliticalCartoons.com. Copyright © 2011 by John Cole, www.PoliticalCartoons.com. All rights reserved. Reproduced by permission.

of executions. Over one-third of Texas's 305 death row inmates—and half of the state's 121 black death row prisoners—are from Harris County. One of those African Americans, Duane Buck, was sentenced based on the testimony of an expert psychologist who maintained that blacks are prone to violence. In 2008, Harris County district attorney Chuck Rosenthal resigned after sending an e-mail message titled "fatal overdose", featuring a photo of a black man lying on the ground surrounded by watermelons and a bucket of chicken.

Race and Capital Punishment Go Hand in Hand in the United States

But this is nothing new: Race and capital punishment in the US have always been inseparable. According to the Washington-based Death Penalty Information Center (DPIC),

56% of death row inmates are black or Hispanic. However, although racial minorities comprise half of all murder victims nationwide, a far greater proportion (77%) of the victims in capital convictions were white. The racial identity of the murder victim is thus a leading factor in determining who receives a death sentence in America. Amnesty International also reports that 20% of blacks nationwide were convicted by all-white juries.

Given the over-representation of black and Hispanic prisoners on death row, it is hardly surprising that of the 139 capital convicts found innocent since 1973, 61% have been of color.

The disparities multiply: Nationally, Alabama ranks 23rd in population, but second in executions in 2011. In Alabama, African Americans are 27% of the population, yet comprise 63% of the prisoners. And while 65% of murders involve black victims, 80% of death sentences involve white victims. Further, according to the Equal Justice Initiative, 60% of black death row prisoners were convicted of killing a white person, although cases involving black defendants and white murder victims represent a mere 6% of the murders in Alabama.

In the past 10 years, 23 Alabama death penalty cases have been overturned because prosecutors had illegally struck black people from the juries. Alabama has no black appellate judges, and only one black prosecutor. And nationally, 98% of prosecutors are white.

Location Is a Factor in Racial Bias

If the death penalty is highly racialised, it is a regional and local phenomenon as well. Over three-quarters of executions take place in the states of the former Confederacy (including 35% in Texas alone) with their history of racial violence, lynching and arbitrary Black Codes and Jim Crow laws, which sanctioned death for blacks for certain offenses.

In death penalty states, the decision to seek the death penalty takes place on the county level at the discretion of the district attorney. Only 10% of the 3,148 counties in America have returned a single death sentence; a mere 1% of counties returned one or more death sentences per year.

According to data from DPIC, 15 US counties accounted for 30% of the executions since 1976—which is less than 1% of counties in the country, and less than 1% of the total counties in all death penalty states. Nine of these counties are in Texas, and three are in Alabama.

Capital punishment has national and international implications, yet in the US—where a very small number of counties, largely in the South, accounts for a majority of the executions—local officials enjoy broad powers to prosecute and execute based on groundless assumptions and bias about race. Questions of guilt and innocence are subordinated to expediency and prejudice.

> *"It would be naïve to suggest that racism has been eliminated in the United States; but it would be equally mistaken to suggest that nothing has changed."*

Racial Bias in the Capital Punishment System Has Decreased over Time

Charles Lane

Charles Lane is a contributor to the Washington Post *and author of* Stay of Execution: Saving the Death Penalty from Itself. *In the following viewpoint, Lane argues that death penalty opponents have encouraged doubts about the manner in which the death penalty is administered as a way to unfairly sway public opinion about capital punishment. Citing statistical data from several studies, Lane asserts that while racial discrimination has not been eliminated, progress has been made as it relates to the death penalty system. Lane also describes how landmark cases such as* Furman v. Georgia *have helped to change the racial composition of death row. Lane concludes that election outcomes, jury decisions, and demographics indicate that blacks are effectively using their power to curb capital punishment.*

As you read, consider the following questions:

1. According to a Gallup poll cited by Lane, what percentage of Americans say the death penalty is not imposed often enough?

2. What percentage of those executed since the 1976 case *Gregg v. Georgia* have been white, according to Lane?

3. How many of the sixty-six murderers sentenced to death in Maryland after 1978 were eventually executed, according to Lane?

The death penalty is back in the news [in November/ December 2010]. In the past month alone, Virginia has executed a woman for her role in the murder-for-hire of her husband and stepson, despite claims that she was nearly mentally retarded. States have grappled with a looming shortage of lethal injection drugs. A federal court in Georgia has rebuffed a death row inmate's claim that he is an innocent man, falsely convicted—but defense lawyers insist the judge got it wrong. And in North Carolina, the vast majority of that state's 156 death row inmates have filed appeals based on a new law that permits them to challenge their sentences on grounds of racial bias.

For opponents of the death penalty, these and other events add up to more evidence that capital punishment in the United States is, in the words of one prominent study, "a broken system." Of course, even a smoothly functioning death penalty would, in their view, violate basic human decency and basic human rights. Their emphasis on capital punishment's operational flaws is a concession to political reality. According to Gallup, 65 percent of Americans favor the use of the death penalty for a person convicted of murder. Half of Americans say the death penalty is not imposed often enough; only 20 percent say it is imposed too often. So opponents' best hope is to encourage doubts about the way it is implemented—an approach that offers the public a way to be against the death penalty, *as it exists in the United States today*, without necessarily ruling it out in principle.

Statistical Data May Show Progress

Racial bias ranks high on the list of accusations. There's a good reason for this: Racial disparities in capital sentencing are an historical reality—and a particularly ugly one at that. Anyone who doubts the death penalty's past connection with racism need only consider this statistic: Between 1930 and 1967 (at which point executions stopped pending a decade-long Supreme Court overhaul of the death penalty), 54 percent of the 3,859 people put to death under civilian authority in the U.S. were African American. This was not only out of proportion with the black share of the total population but also out of proportion with the percentage of serious crimes committed by blacks. Given that history, lingering racism is an undeniable risk factor looming over today's system.

The question, however, is whether that risk is actually as large and as ineradicable as conventional wisdom maintains. And the answer is: probably not. In fact, much of the statistical evidence cited by death penalty critics to show that blacks and whites fare differently in capital cases does not necessarily prove racism at all. To the contrary, it could well reflect racial progress.

Historical Racial Bias in Death Penalty States

In the past, the disproportionate impact of capital punishment against blacks reflected racism all across the country, but especially in the Southern states, which used execution to enforce a broader caste system. The South put blacks to death for rape far more often than whites—especially when the alleged victim was a white woman. Of the 455 men executed for rape in the United States between 1930 and 1967, 90 percent were African American.

These appalling facts formed the background for the Supreme Court's consideration of the death penalty in the 1960s and 1970s. It was no accident that the Legal Defense [and Educational] Fund of the National Association for the Advancement of Colored People, known as the LDF, led the constitutional challenges. The litigation culminated in a 1972 case, *Furman v. Georgia*, in which the Supreme Court struck down all existing state death penalty laws. Two of the three cases grouped under that title involved African American men sentenced to death for raping white women in the South. The third was a black man convicted of killing a white man in the course of a bungled burglary.

Furman v. Georgia Had a Lasting Impact on Reducing Racism

To be sure, the Supreme Court did not explicitly confront racial disparities during this period; it refused even to hear the argument that the discriminatory death penalty for rape violated the 14th Amendment guarantee of equal treatment under state law. However, in *Furman*, at least one justice in the majority, William O. Douglas, opined that racial disparities were part of what made the death penalty "cruel and unusual" under the 8th Amendment, and other justices alluded to race in their analyses of the penalty's arbitrariness. "Race discrimination was not formally part of *Furman*, and Douglas was the only justice who emphasized it," writes Professor Stuart Banner of the University of California at Los Angeles law school, a death penalty historian. "But everyone knew it was lurking not far beneath the surface."

Furman left room for states to reinstate capital punishment—if they could purge their laws of the general lack of consistent standards, racial or otherwise, upon which the court had based its constitutional ruling. The states did so by requiring juries to weigh the defendant's sentence separately from his guilt or innocence, and, in this "sentencing trial," to take account of both "aggravating" evidence that supported the death penalty and "mitigating" evidence that argued against it. In 1976, the court approved of the changes, in a case known as *Gregg v. Georgia*. A three-justice plurality concluded that the revisions "narrowed the class of murderers subject to capital punishment" and "minimize[d] the risk of wholly arbitrary and capricious action," thus curing the ills identified in *Furman*.

Though usually remembered as the court's failed attempt to abolish the death penalty, *Furman* nevertheless had a lasting impact, rendering capital punishment less blatantly racist than it had been in the past. Most new state laws adopted in response to *Furman* omitted rape as a capital crime. *Gregg* provided at least some assurance that jurors would consider an individual defendant's disadvantages in life, including those related to racial discrimination. Even more importantly, perhaps, *Gregg* created a basis for condemned men to claim on appeal that their juries had failed to consider such "mitigating" factors.

And finally, the court followed up *Gregg* in 1977 by banning the death penalty for rape of an adult woman, albeit in a decision that emphasized not race but society's evolving notions of the appropriate punishment for such crimes. Though only Georgia still prescribed death for rape at that point, the court seemed determined to make sure it never came back.

Court Cases Have Led to Changes on Death Row

Taken together, these changes helped transform the racial composition of death row. Whereas some 54 percent of those executed between 1930 and 1967 were black, as we have seen, 56 percent of those executed in the post-*Gregg* era have been white, while 35 percent have been black and 9 percent have been Latinos and other minorities. In other words, the African American share of executions dropped by a third. Whites also make up the largest portion of those sentenced to death during the post-*Gregg* period.

To be sure, this did not necessarily mean that racial imbalances had been eliminated. African Americans were still overrepresented on death row relative to their share of the population. And, in the aftermath of *Gregg*, death penalty critics discovered a new—but to them no less troubling—racial pattern in sentencing. The disparity involved not the race of the defendant, but the race of the victim. In a famous LDF-funded study of 2,484 murder cases in Georgia between 1973 and 1979, Professor David Baldus of the University of Iowa showed that, even after taking account of 39 nonracial variables, defendants charged with killing whites were 4.3 times as likely to receive the death penalty as defendants charged with killing blacks. Within the category of those who killed whites, black defendants were 10 percent more likely to receive a death sentence than were whites.

Armed with the Baldus study, the LDF took another shot at persuading the Supreme Court that the death penalty was hopelessly infected with arbitrary considerations such as race, even in Georgia, whose new statute the court had specifically approved in *Gregg*. Of course, the argument had extra plausibility in a Southern state that had recently emerged from a racist past. To the LDF, Baldus's statistics showed that, consciously or not, Georgia's legal apparatus placed a higher value on white life than black life, and thus punished murder of whites more harshly than murder of blacks, especially when a black man had the effrontery to kill a white person.

In a 1987 case, *McCleskey v. Kemp*, the court rejected this claim by a vote of 5-4. For the majority, Justice Lewis F. Powell wrote that the LDF had failed to show discriminatory intent by Georgia officials, and that the court could not infer unconstitutional motives from Baldus's statistics. "We decline to assume that what is unexplained is invidious," Justice Powell wrote. To hold otherwise, Justice Powell added, would undermine the entire justice system by rendering unconstitutional any statistical disparity in sentencing, capital or otherwise, among ethnic groups, men and women, or even attractive defendants and unattractive ones.

Studies Do Not Necessarily Reflect Racism

McCleskey foreclosed constitutional challenges based on statistics such as those in Baldus's study, but it could not stop Baldus and others from continuing their research. They went on to produce additional studies showing similar race-of-the-victim disparities in states across the country. Most death row inmates fighting their sentences in North Carolina today have cited a study by Michigan State [University] law professors (including a former student of Baldus) showing that killers of whites are more than twice as likely to get death as killers of blacks.

As a result, *McCleskey* has acquired a bad reputation; some legal academics liken it to the 1857 *Dred Scott* decision [referring to *Dred Scott v. Sandford*] that said people of African ancestry could not claim U.S. citizenship. After retiring from the court, Justice Powell himself told a biographer that he regretted his opinion in the case.

But Justice Powell may have been excessively self-critical. Though statistical research confirms Baldus's observations, it does not necessarily support the interpretation of the data that death penalty opponents advanced in *McCleskey*—and still advance today. The fact that killers of whites have been more likely to receive the death penalty since *Gregg* does not necessarily reflect racism of the kind that pervaded the pre-*Furman* system; it does not necessarily reflect racism at all.

Statistical Data Counters Some Common Assumptions

This assessment begins by acknowledging that African Americans commit a disproportionate number of murders in the United States: approximately half, according to government statistics. Yet in the death penalty states of post-*Gregg* America, black murderers have actually been somewhat *less likely* to wind up on death row than their white counterparts. Blacks committed 51.5 percent of murders nationwide between 1976 and 1998, according to a 2004 study by Cornell [University] law professors John Blume, Theodore Eisenberg and Martin T. Wells, but accounted for only 41.3 percent of those sentenced to death from 1977 to 1999. This relationship held true in every death penalty state, and—contrary to conventional wisdom—the underrepresentation of blacks on death row was *greatest* in the South. Only California, Utah and Nevada came close to sentencing black murderers to death in proportion to their share of the total.

The Cornell law professors (who oppose the death penalty) confirmed Baldus's research in the sense that they also detected what they called "a racial hierarchy" in capital sentencing. Blacks charged with killing blacks were sentenced to death less often than whites charged with killing whites, and blacks charged with killing whites were sentenced to death most frequently of all.

Race, however, "tugs in two different directions," they argued. The higher likelihood of a death sentence for black killers of whites tends to increase the black share of death row. The lower likelihood of a death sentence for black killers of blacks tends to decrease it. And the second effect is far larger than the first, since blacks are far more likely to kill other blacks than they are to kill whites. As the Cornell law professors put it, "Interracial crime is the exception, not the rule." Therefore, the relative lack of black killers of blacks on death row "swamps" the relative excess of black killers of whites and largely explains the underrepresentation of black murderers among those sentenced to death.

Black-on-Black Homicides Are Rarely Death Penalty Cases

That leaves the question of why black-on-black murder so seldom results in the death penalty. One possibility is that these killings are less likely than others to take place during the commission of an additional crime, such as rape, robbery or kidnapping, which is the usual standard for aggravated or capital murder under state death penalty statutes. According to recent data assembled by the nonprofit Violence Policy Center in Washington, DC, black-victim homicides rarely include additional crimes. In 2006, for example, there was no other felony in 69 percent of the black-victim homicides for which the circumstances could be identified. The typical scenario, the study showed, was an argument between friends, family members, or acquaintances that escalated until someone impulsively reached for a gun and shot the victim.

According to the Cornell law professors, the main factor is the reluctance of local prosecutors to seek the death penalty in black-on-black homicides. What accounts for that reluctance? While not dismissing the possibility that white prosecutors—consciously or not—placed a lower value on black life, the Cornell professors emphasized another reason: prosecutorial realism. Above all, prosecutors do not seek the death penalty unless they think they can actually persuade a jury to impose it. In jurisdictions with large African American populations, where most black-on-black crime occurs, persuading a jury to sentence a defendant to death is relatively difficult. As much survey data confirms, African Americans are the one U.S. demographic group that largely opposes the death penalty, no doubt because of its terrible historical impact on blacks in the South. Also, in jurisdictions where elected prosecutors must appeal to black voters, prosecutors are that much less likely to support capital punishment.

Racial Progress Is Reflected in Elections, Juries, and Demographics

This is how race-of-the-victim disparities can be said to reflect racial progress. After all, blacks neither voted in elections nor served on juries in substantial numbers, especially in the South, until the late 1960s. Now that they do, they appear to be using this power to limit capital punishment in the cases closest to them. In a separate study, published in 2005, Eisenberg found support for this hypothesis in county-level data for five death penalty states—Georgia, Maryland, Pennsylvania, South Carolina and Virginia. The death sentence rate in black defendant/black victim homicides decreased as the percentage of blacks in a county's population increased. "This suggests that minority community skepticism about the justness of the death penalty is a contributing factor to low death sentence rates" in black-on-black murder cases, Eisenberg concluded.

Maryland presents a particularly suggestive case. Its pre-*Furman* death penalty practices resembled those of the South. A significant portion of its executions prior to 1972—about a third—came in rape cases. Maryland reestablished the death penalty after *Gregg* in a 1978 statute that omitted the death penalty for rape and specified first-degree murder with certain aggravating factors as the only death-eligible crime. Since then, Maryland has not been a major locus of the death penalty; despite its relatively high murder rate, the state sentenced only 66 murderers to death after 1978. Of those, only five were eventually executed (the first in 1994), and five remain on death row.

The other thing that happened in post-*Gregg* Maryland was the rise of black majorities in the city of Baltimore and in Prince George's County, a suburb of Washington, DC. These two jurisdictions account for the vast majority of homicides in the state, most of which involve both black victims and perpetrators. Yet public officials in both jurisdictions have generally eschewed the death penalty, consistent with their own views and the views of their constituents (who are also potential jurors). Baltimore city prosecutors last sought and won the death penalty in 1998 in a single case that was later overturned on appeal. The last Prince George's County death sentence occurred in 1996.

Racism Still Exists, but Statistical Data Points to Progress

The situation could not have been more different in Baltimore County, a 75 percent white suburb adjacent to the city of Baltimore. During most of the post-*Gregg* period, the county's chief prosecutor adhered to a policy of seeking the death penalty in every eligible case. Ironically enough, she did so to avoid any appearance of racial discrimination; her view was that she could never be accused of exercising prosecutorial discretion in a discriminatory manner if she never exercised it at all.

Given Baltimore County's relatively large population (750,000 in 2005) and its white majority—which meant that most homicide victims were white—and given the polar opposite policies pursued by its black-majority neighbors, it is no wonder that Maryland's death penalty was meted out more frequently to killers of whites. But this was a consequence of county-level politics and demography, not statewide racial discrimination. Indeed, much if not most of the racial and jurisdictional imbalance in Maryland's death penalty may demonstrate the increased power of black citizens during the post-*Gregg* era. Most African Americans in Maryland, like most African Americans generally, oppose the death penalty; and where they live, it has been abolished de facto.

It would be naïve to suggest that racism has been eliminated in the United States; but it would be equally mistaken to suggest that nothing has changed. To the extent that death penalty foes do the latter, they are misinterpreting the data and misleading public opinion.

> "DNA testing has exposed some gaping
> flaws in the system, calling into ques-
> tion traditional assumptions on the
> value of eyewitness testimony, forensic
> evidence, confessions, and the appeals
> process."

DNA Testing Reveals Serious Problems in the Capital Punishment System

Radley Balko

Radley Balko was a policy analyst for the Cato Institute and a senior editor at Reason *magazine; he is a contributor to numerous publications and media outlets. In the following viewpoint, Balko asserts that DNA testing has revealed some major shortcomings of the capital punishment system, raising serious questions about how many innocents have been wrongfully convicted and how many are now sitting in prison. He contends that prosecutors and others involved in the criminal justice system have historically used "absurd math" to determine wrongful conviction rates. As a result, Balko says, some have incorrectly concluded that there is nothing wrong with the way the current capital punishment system is working.*

Radley Balko, "How Many More Are Innocent?," Reason.com, February 8, 2010. Reproduced by permission.

As you read, consider the following questions:

1. What evidence did Justice Antonin Scalia give to refute the idea that an innocent person may have been executed, according to Balko?

2. According to Balko, how many people would be incarcerated given a 2 percent wrongful conviction rate?

3. According to Balko, what conclusions can be reached about the 250 DNA exonerations referred to in the viewpoint?

Freddie Peacock of Rochester, New York, was convicted of rape in 1976. Last week [in February 2010] he became the 250th person to be exonerated by DNA testing since 1989. According to a new report by the Innocence Project, those 250 prisoners served 3,160 years between them; 17 spent time on death row. Remarkably, 67 percent of them were convicted after 2000—a decade after the onset of modern DNA testing. The glaring question here is, *How many more are there?*

Calculating the percentage of innocents now in prison is a tricky and controversial process. The numerator itself is difficult enough to figure out. The certainty of DNA testing means we can be positive the 250 cases listed in the Innocence Project report didn't commit the crimes for which they were convicted, and that number also continues to rise. But there are hundreds of other cases in which convictions have been overturned due to a lack of evidence, recantation of eyewitness testimony, or police or prosecutorial misconduct, but for which there was no DNA evidence to establish definitive guilt or innocence. Those were wrongful convictions in that there wasn't sufficient evidence to establish reasonable doubt, but we can't be sure all the accused were factually innocent.

Most prosecutors fight requests for post-conviction DNA testing. That means the discovery of wrongful convictions is limited by the time and resources available to the Innocence

Project and similar legal aid organizations to fight for a test in court. It's notable that in one of the few jurisdictions where the district attorney is actively seeking out wrongful convictions—Dallas County, Texas—the county by itself has seen more exonerations than all but a handful of individual states. If prosecutors in other jurisdictions were to follow Dallas D.A. Craig Watkins' lead, that 250 figure would be significantly higher.

Wrongful Conviction Rates Appear to Be Miscalculated

If the numerator is tough to figure, the denominator is even more controversial. One of the more farcical attempts at writing off the growing number of DNA exonerations came in a concurring opinion that Supreme Court justice Antonin Scalia wrote in the 2005 case *Kansas v. Marsh*. Scalia began by dismissing the idea that an innocent person may have been executed in America, explaining that if such a tragedy had occurred, "we would not have to hunt for it; the innocent's name would be shouted from the rooftops by the abolition lobby."

Scalia has probably since become acquainted with the name Cameron Todd Willingham, the Texas man executed in 2004 who was likely innocent. But the justice's pique also betrays an unfamiliarity with how death penalty opposition organizations work. While Scalia is right that proof of an executed innocent would be good rhetorical fodder for death penalty abolitionists, legal aid groups aren't about to waste their limited resources hunting down mistaken executions when there are living, breathing innocents still to be discovered. Moreover, in many jurisdictions, prosecutors destroy the case files after an execution, making any post-execution investigation rather difficult. That we don't know for certain about more executed innocents doesn't mean they haven't happened.

DNA Testing Proved Kirk Bloodsworth's Innocence

The only reason my name was cleared is because prosecutors agreed to test the evidence. I am living proof that when scientific evidence is available, there is simply no excuse to refuse testing.

Kirk Bloodsworth,
"Texas Must Test DNA Before Carrying Out Skinner Execution,"
Huffington Post, *October 28, 2011. www.huffingtonpost.com.*

Scalia then cited some absurd math from Josh Marquis, an Oregon prosecutor who has held various executive positions for the National District Attorneys Association. According to the Marquis formula Scalia endorsed, at the time there had been about 200 DNA exonerations. For posterity, Marquis then arbitrarily multiplied that number by 10, to come up with 2,000 wrongful convictions. Marquis then took *every single felony conviction over the previous 15 years* as his denominator, to come up with a meager .027 wrongful conviction rate. Move along, America. Nothing to see here. Your criminal justice system's performing just fine.

The figure is absurd. First, the subset of cases for which DNA testing can prove guilt is exceedingly small. It's generally limited to most rape and some murder cases. You can throw out the entire body of drug charges and nearly all burglary, robbery, assault, and other classes of felonies. As University of Michigan law professor Samuel L. Gross wrote of Marquis in a 2008 article in the *Annual Review of Law and Social Science,* "By this logic, we could estimate the proportion of baseball players who've used steroids by dividing the number of major league players who've been caught by the total of all baseball players at all levels: major league, minor league, semipro, college and Little League—and maybe throwing in football and basketball players as well."

If the aim is to calculate the percentage of people who *claim* they're innocent and who actually are, you might throw out all cases decided by a guilty plea, too. But this can also get tricky. According to the Innocence Project, more than a quarter of DNA exonerations included a false confession or guilty plea. The plea bargaining process can also induce innocent people to plead guilty to lesser crimes to avoid charges with more serious prison time, particularly in drug cases.

DNA Testing Shows That Wrongful Convictions Happen

The Innocence Project cites a study by Seton Hall's D. Michael Risinger that puts the percentage of innocents in prison at 3 to 5 percent. But that study looked only at capital crimes, and there's yet more debate over whether data gleaned from those accused of crimes that are eligible for the death penalty would translate into higher or lower wrongful conviction rates for those accused of lesser crimes. (Those who argue that it would be higher note that there's more pressure on prosecutors and jurors to hold someone accountable in murder cases. On the other hand, defendants tend to have better representation in capital cases.) But even dropping below the study's floor, using the 2008 prison population, a 2 percent wrongful conviction rate would mean about 46,000 people [were] incarcerated for crimes they didn't commit.

Whatever the percentage, DNA testing has exposed some gaping flaws in the system, calling into question traditional assumptions on the value of eyewitness testimony, forensic evidence, confessions, and the appeals process. (In several cases in which a defendant was later exonerated by DNA testing, appeals courts not only upheld convictions, but also noted the "overwhelming evidence" of the defendants' guilt.) Scalia stated in *Marsh* that an exoneration "demonstrates not the failure of the system but its success," but it would be naïve to believe the same systemic flaws exposed by these exonerations in the small subset of cases for which DNA testing is available don't also exist in the much larger pool of non-DNA cases. Put another way, if we now know because of DNA testing that misconduct by police and prosecutors produced a wrongful conviction in a high-profile murder case, it's probably safe to assume that the same problems led to the wrongful conviction of a number of routine drug suspects over the years, too. The difference is that there's no test to clear those people's names.

So these 250 DNA exonerations aren't proof that the system is working. They're a wake-up call that it isn't. Instead of falling back on groups like the Innocence Project to serve as unofficial checks against wrongful convictions, lawmakers, judges, and law enforcement officials should be looking at why there's so much work for these organizations in the first place.

> "DNA will not solve the problem of wrongful death penalty convictions. It is quite limited because it is not present in the great majority of murder cases."

DNA Testing Cannot Solve Fundamental Flaws in the Capital Punishment System

Juan Roberto Meléndez-Colón

In the following viewpoint, Juan Roberto Meléndez-Colón, a former inmate, talks about how he was released from death row based on evidence that did not involve DNA testing. Meléndez-Colón explains that based on shaky testimony, he was wrongfully convicted and sentenced to death for allegedly robbing and murdering a man. More than seventeen years later, he reports, he was exonerated and released from Florida's death row after a taped confession from the real killer surfaced. According to Meléndez-Colón, DNA testing will not resolve many wrongful conviction cases because no such evidence exists in a great number of them. He adds that abolishing the death penalty in the state of New Hampshire would save taxpayer money that could be better spent on public safety to protect citizens from real criminals.

Juan Roberto Meléndez-Colón, "A Story for N.H. from Death Row," Witness to Innocence, February 5, 2010. www.witnesstoinnocence.org. Copyright © 2010 by Witness to Innocence. All rights reserved. Reproduced by permission.

As you read, consider the following questions:

1. How many death row exonerations involved DNA, according to Meléndez-Colón?

2. What does Meléndez-Colón say that he would say to those who say we need to shorten the appeals process to make the death penalty less expensive?

3. Who was Frank Lee Smith, according to Meléndez-Colón?

I was born in Brooklyn, N.Y., and raised on the island of Puerto Rico. I came to the United States as a young man to try to make a better life for myself, in search of the American dream. Instead, I lived the American nightmare.

In 1984, I was convicted and sentenced to death in Florida for a crime I did not commit. It was a brutal crime, a robbery and murder of a white man—Delbert Baker. He was known as "Mr. Del." He was shot three times and his throat was slashed. The crime scene was drenched in blood. There was a rush to find someone accountable for this horrendous crime and in that rush, the rules were broken.

Seventeen years, eight months and one day later, on January 3, 2002, I was exonerated and released from death row.

At that time, I became the 99th person in the United States to be released from death row with evidence of innocence since 1973. Today [in February 2010], there are 139 of us. I suppose you could call us "the lucky ones." I wonder how many of the 1,193 who have already been executed, were not so lucky and were executed in spite of their innocence?

DNA Does Not Solve Wrongful Death Penalty Convictions

My case did not involve DNA. In fact, of the 139 death row exonerations, only 17 of them involved DNA. DNA will not solve the problem of wrongful death penalty convictions. It is quite limited because it is not present in the great majority of murder cases.

DNA Testing Is Often Ineffective

Post-conviction DNA testing, more often than not, provides either inconclusive results or, in many cases, confirms the guilt of the prisoner seeking testing. In addition, DNA testing is costly, time-consuming, and provides an additional administrative burden on already overextended state criminal justice systems.

Gwendolyn Carroll, "Proven Guilty: An Examination of the Penalty-Free World of Post-Conviction DNA Testing," Journal of Criminal Law and Criminology, vol. 97, no. 2, January 1, 2007.

I was convicted and sentenced to death based on the testimony of two questionable witnesses. There was no physical evidence against me. Had it not been for the fortunate discovery of the taped confession of the real killer—16 years after I had been sentenced to death—I would not be sharing my story with you today. When all was said and done, it was discovered that the real killer confessed to about 20 people. I was not saved by the system. I was saved in spite of the system.

For those who would say we need to shorten the appeals process to make the death penalty less expensive, I would ask them to look at my case. . . .

Lastly, I'd like to share a story with you about a good friend of mine on death row. Frank Lee Smith. A black man. Frank was on death row for 14 years. He always claimed that he was innocent. He became sick and was dying of cancer. He begged the state of Florida to do the DNA testing. He said the tests would show that he was innocent. Unfortunately, by the time the results came in, it was too late for Frank. He died of cancer before the tests showed that he did not commit the crime. And it was also too late for several young women who became victims of the real killer. While Frank was on death row, the real killer could not stop killing. You see, this is not a system that protects our communities, it does not protect our children and it does not protect our law enforcement officers. When an innocent man is on death row, the real killer is most likely out on the streets, free to kill again. The huge amount of money that could be saved by getting rid of the death penalty in New Hampshire could be used to get it right—to protect the public from the real perpetrators. It could be used instead by your law enforcement departments, for better training, to give your police officers the tools they need to properly investigate violent crime, to put the dangerous people behind bars where they belong and to develop programs that will reduce violence in your communities.

The Death Penalty Is Costly and Unnecessary

Sometimes we hear people say that those who commit horrible crimes deserve the death penalty. I think they've got it backwards. The question is not whether they deserve the death penalty; the question is whether we deserve the death penalty. Does New Hampshire deserve the death penalty? That is what I would ask you to consider. And I think the answer is clear.

New Hampshire does not deserve a law that is cruel and unnecessary—you have the alternative of life without the possibility of parole.

New Hampshire does not deserve a law that costs too much. The money saved by abolishing the death penalty and replacing it with life without the possibility of parole can be directed instead to New Hampshire's public safety departments where it can be used to reduce violence in your communities.

Finally, New Hampshire does not deserve a law that can kill an innocent person. The death penalty is a law that is made by human beings and carried out by human beings, and we all know that human beings make mistakes. Once the punishment of death has been imposed, it can never be reversed. As my dear friend, another death row exoneree, Freddie Pitts, has said: You can always release an innocent person from prison—from a sentence of life without parole—but you can never release an innocent man from the grave.

For these reasons, I ask you to recommend that the legislature of the state of New Hampshire abolish the death penalty.

| *"The death penalty is not the answer to the problem of violence committed by persons with severe mental illness."*

People with Mental Illness Should Be Exempt from the Death Penalty

Susannah Sheffer

Susannah Sheffer is a staff writer and project director for the Massachusetts-based nonprofit Murder Victims' Families for Human Rights; she has written a number of materials about opposition to the death penalty. She also has authored and coauthored several books, including In a Dark Time: A Prisoner's Struggle for Healing and Change. *In this viewpoint, Sheffer asserts that the death penalty is not an appropriate punishment for severely mentally ill individuals who commit murder. Sheffer also points to the disturbing questions that such crimes raise about the failure of societal responsibility in addressing warning signs that can lead to such tragedies. It is a cruel irony, Sheffer says, that an individual suffering from severe mental illness often only receives needed help following a tragedy, leaving victims' families to wonder what, if anything, could have been done to prevent the crime in the first place.*

As you read, consider the following questions:

1. From what illness did Andrew Goldstein suffer, according to Sheffer?

2. Why does Barbara McNally, as quoted in the viewpoint, say she was opposed to the death penalty?

3. How old was Tom Lowenstein when his father was killed, according to the viewpoint?

In its 2006 report, "USA: The Execution of Mentally Ill Offenders," Amnesty International suggests that murders committed by people with severe mental illness raise questions of societal responsibility—and failure of responsibility—in a particularly vivid way. In a section titled "Burying Society's Mistakes," Amnesty's report suggests that

> In some cases involving mentally impaired defendants, there are indications that individuals within wider society failed to heed warnings that could have averted a tragedy. This is not to suggest that crimes committed by mentally impaired people are to be condoned or excused. It is, however, to ask whether society could devote its energies and resources more constructively.

In the aftermath of their incomparable loss, murder victims' families find themselves thrust into the complex territory between not condoning or excusing an individual act and being forced to understand that the individual may be in some sense less than fully responsible for that act. The territory is complicated further when victims' families grasp the possibility that others might have been able to foresee and even prevent the act. What were the warning signs? Who or what agency failed to heed them? What might have been done differently?

For some, the pursuit of answers to these questions eventually coalesces into a determined advocacy for specific ways in which society might better dedicate its resources to help people with mental illness, thereby preventing further loss of life. But at the outset, the focus of these shocked and grieving family members is simply on trying to make sense of what had happened.

Mental Illness Impacts Victims' Families

When Pat Webdale got a frantic phone call from her daughter Kim saying that the younger Webdale sister, Kendra, had been killed in the New York City subway, Pat struggled to absorb what she was hearing. At first the family thought Kendra had fallen accidentally onto the subway tracks. Then they learned that she had been pushed and they guessed that she was the victim of an attempted mugging. Finally the news came that Kendra had been pushed by a man named Andrew Goldstein who was quickly revealed to be suffering from schizophrenia.

"I didn't really know anything about real mental illness," Pat recalls. "My family went to Barnes and Noble almost immediately [after getting the news], and that's when we started learning." Right away Pat struggled with the tension between "needing a consequence," as she summarized it, and believing that Andrew Goldstein "didn't know what he was doing." She didn't want to see Goldstein out on the street again, and as she learned that he had assaulted 13 people prior to his fatal assault on Kendra, she "felt like, why didn't somebody see what he needed 13 times ago?"

Like Pat Webdale, Linda Gregory knew little about mental illness before its effects invaded her life. Linda's husband, Gene Gregory, a deputy sheriff in Seminole County, Florida, had occasionally been called in to try to defuse a potentially volatile situation involving someone with mental illness. Linda remembers that after those encounters he "would come home and say something about inadequate services and how somebody should do something to help law enforcement be able to do more." Linda sometimes worried for her husband's safety;

her only experience with mental illness was of a friend of her brother's when they were all growing up. "I remember us just calling him 'crazy.' Truthfully, other than that, I was ignorant; I knew nothing else about mental illness."

On the day of his murder in 1998, Deputy Gregory had been called in to assist when Alan Singletary, diagnosed years earlier with paranoid schizophrenia, pulled a gun on the landlord who had threatened to evict him. During a 13-hour standoff, Alan Singletary shot and killed Deputy Gregory and wounded two other deputies. Alan Singletary himself was then killed by gunfire from the other deputies who had come to assist.

Linda remembers the long night of waiting for news:

> They had come to get me to take me to the hospital—they knew my husband was down but they didn't know how badly he was injured. On the way, they learned that they weren't able to get in to him, so they took me to the sheriff's office. Friends came and we had a vigil there and prayer and that kind of thing. Nothing was said at that time about the man's mental illness. In the wee hours, the sheriff came in. He never had to tell me [that Gene was dead] because when I saw him coming in the door I knew.

Initially, Linda's main concern was reaching her grown children quickly so that they wouldn't have to learn of their father's death from a news report. In the midst of the family's fresh shock and grief, the seeds of Linda's later activism were already being sown:

> Early the next morning, Sheriff Eslinger came to see me and he told me a little about Alan because he had talked to Alice, his sister. He told me, "I've been so concerned about mental illness and there's been nothing much we could do, but I promise you today that we're going to make a difference."

A History of Mental Illness

In the ensuing weeks, Linda learned that after the murder, Alan Singletary's sister had sent a letter to the sheriff describing how the family had tried for years to get help for her brother. "They couldn't get much help for him," Linda says, summarizing the letter, "and they knew something like this would eventually happen."

Alan Singletary's history of mental illness was reported in the early news coverage of the standoff. Similarly, news coverage of the murder of Laura Wilcox, in California, immediately focused on the issue of mental illness because the murder took place at a behavioral health clinic where Laura, a college student, was working as a receptionist during her winter break in 2001. Laura was killed when Scott Thorpe, a patient of the clinic, approached the glass window separating the receptionist from the waiting room and fired four shots at close range.

Laura's mother, Amanda Wilcox, describes herself as "in shock, numb, practically non-functional" when the family first got the news of Laura's murder. But the tragedy "turned very soon to issues of mental health," recalls Laura's father, Nick Wilcox. If Scott Thorpe was a patient of the clinic, did that mean he was under supervised treatment? How did it happen that his family's warning calls to the clinic weren't returned, or that the psychiatrist had written six months earlier that he was dangerous and should be hospitalized but Scott Thorpe was still living alone in a house full of assault weapons?

"We had an ongoing need for information and we couldn't get it," Amanda recalls of the period immediately after Laura's murder. "I thought after something like this, someone comes and tells you what happened. It's like we didn't exist for the county. We had made an initial claim [against the county] and that's how we got the police report, which had a lot in it relating to the mental health of Scott Thorpe. It was obvious to us that there was a problem."

Legal Protections Are Needed for Mentally Ill Defendants

In 2006, the American Bar Association passed a resolution calling for the exemption of those with serious mental illness from imposition and execution of the death penalty. At the time of this writing [in 2009], Connecticut is the only state that prohibits the execution of someone who is mentally ill. . . .

Most importantly, we will create a criminal justice system that comes closer to ensuring that the punishment fits the crime and the defendant.

"Mental Illness and the Death Penalty,"
American Civil Liberties Union, May 5, 2009.
www.aclu.org.

From Grief to Activism

These families eventually became activists on the issue of mental health reform, and their activism grew out of what they learned from looking back to the period before the tragedy to try to determine how it had come to happen, and then looking forward to what policy reforms seemed to be needed. The possibility of the death penalty as a response to their losses struck these families as not only inappropriate but, even more specifically, as a way of bypassing any attempt to understand what had led to the murder.

In the period immediately following Laura Wilcox's murder, a newspaper article quoted the district attorney stating that he would seek the death penalty for Scott Thorpe. Shortly thereafter, the Wilcoxes publicly expressed their opposition to the death penalty. Nick recalls the eventual conversation that he and Amanda had with the DA [district attorney]:

We met with the district attorney about six months later and affirmed that we don't seek the death penalty in our name. He said, "You know, I was really upset when I made my initial statement to the paper," but he went on to say that he would not pursue the death penalty now.

The Wilcoxes' opposition to the death penalty was part moral—as they later said in several public statements, "To execute him for an act he committed while delusional with a severe disease is, to us, simply wrong"—and part driven by their desire to keep the focus on "policy, not vengeance," as Nick says now.

It is common for victims' families to be called upon to state their position on the death penalty to prosecutors or to members of the press. Charlie Strobel, whose mother was killed in Tennessee by an escapee from a prison mental health ward, remembers his family's meeting with the DA:

> The DA's office contacted us and said, "We want to seek the death penalty." I said, "As a family we would not want to seek the death penalty." Our public statement had already said that we agree society needs to be protected from his doing any further harm but we do not wish to seek the death penalty in this matter; it would not be in keeping with the spirit of our mother or with our own wishes. We had said clearly that we were not asking for his release—we had to say that so people wouldn't be out there thinking, "Well, they just want to let him go." So I said to the DA, "As you know, this is what our position is, and I just want to state that again." I said I would do whatever it took, though I don't think I knew what I would do or how I would follow through on that.

Barbara McNally, whose husband, Jim, was killed in Illinois by a childhood friend who was later diagnosed with delusional disorder, would have liked an opportunity to express her opinion on the death penalty directly to the district attorney, but because the man responsible for the murder was never deemed competent to stand trial, the issue of the death penalty was dropped. Initially, however, when Barbara was told that the death penalty was a possibility, she was forced to evaluate where she stood on the issue:

> Early on, shortly following the arraignment, the state did tell me that the charges in the case were severe enough that it comes under the death penalty eligibility. They had 120 days to decide whether they were going to proceed down that path. They did tell me that they were going to talk to me before they made a decision. My feeling was no, I did not want to go down that path. However, I never even got a chance to give that opinion. They just called me and said they weren't going to go for it. I was fine with that, but still [it bothered me that] my opinion didn't matter.
>
> I was opposed to the death penalty because of my faith, my belief that just because he murdered my husband, it is not OK to then go and take his life. But the other main reason was that, let's say, ok, the state goes and kills him, so our family's safe from that one person. How many others are out there? I just didn't see any huge benefit or value. I didn't see that it would really address the problem.

Sentencing the Mentally Ill to Death Does Not Provide Peace of Mind

Linda Gregory discovered through direct experience that the death of the person responsible for her husband's murder didn't make her feel better and didn't, in her view, get to the core of the problem. "I never felt good that Alan Singletary was dead," she said, referring to the fact that the man responsible for her husband's murder had been killed during the same standoff. "I just thought, what a tragedy that might have been prevented. It was a heartbreak for everybody." Years later, Linda's greater understanding of mental illness only underscores for her the futility of executions in such cases:

I wish people who were ignorant like [I was before this happened] would understand that mental illness is an illness; people don't [commit crimes] because they want to. When people aren't able to get the treatment or the services that they need, they can become violent. What good is it going to do to kill someone who is not really responsible for the death? Some people don't understand why I see it this way. They say, "Well, they still did it." Yes, they did it, but they were ill. That's what did it, the illness, so if we combat the illness, and educate the public, then we'll be able to help someone instead of killing them.

Victims' families who did not directly confront the issue of the death penalty in their loved one's case may still find themselves called upon to express an opinion about the issue. Art Laffin, whose brother Paul Laffin was stabbed to death in 1999 by a homeless man as he was leaving the shelter where he had worked for a decade, explains that although the man responsible for the murder was deemed mentally incompetent to stand trial, "It was a very high-profile case and if he had been deemed competent to stand trial, he could have faced the death penalty. My mother said clearly that she would be against such a thing, and I made that clear in my eulogy, too." The Laffins learned that Dennis Soutar had been diagnosed with paranoid schizophrenia years before the murder, and had bounced from shelter to shelter after being released from the hospital. "He fell through the cracks," is how Art describes it.

Hearing or reading a blanket statement assuming that *all* victims' family members support the death penalty can be the lever that propels a survivor to express publicly what had previously been a quietly held belief. Julie Nelson, whose father was murdered by a man who had been diagnosed with schizophrenia, recalls that she wrote a letter to her city's newspaper in response to such an article, and she summarizes her beliefs now by saying, "For me, more killing wouldn't make it any better. To think that one is somehow going to cancel out the other or bring some kind of closure to a tragic event that's already happened doesn't make sense to me and seems to go in the wrong direction."

Tom Lowenstein was 10 years old when his father, Congressman Al Lowenstein, was shot and killed in his office by Dennis Sweeney, who had been diagnosed with paranoid schizophrenia. Tom recalls that he felt compelled to express his opposition to the death penalty publicly when an opinion piece in a Boston newspaper asserted that if you oppose the death penalty, you don't care about victims. Tom disagreed, and he thought, "I can't be the only victims' family member who feels this way, but someone's got to respond to this."

Pat Webdale puts it this way: "Killing another person never brings back the person you lost, and it's like double-doing the crime." Pat traveled to testify against the death penalty in her home state of New York, believing "that they shouldn't be killed, and especially not if they're mentally ill; there are extenuating circumstances and I want treatment in those cases, not an eye for an eye."...

The Death Penalty Does Not Reduce Illness or Violence

In cases of murders committed by individuals with severe mental illness, the available legal outcomes, though all imperfect in the various ways we have outlined here, have one thing in common: They all offer more caution, more mental health intervention, supervision, and scrutiny, and greater protections against further violence than existed regarding the same individuals before they committed a crime. Several of the stories detailed here contain the cruelest of ironies: an individual with mental illness is only now, after committing a murder, receiving the mental health treatment that was so desperately needed in the first place. *Why is this what it took?* the victims' families wonder. In cases that result in an execution, rather than psychiatric commitment or imprisonment, the cruelty of the irony is only compounded: Now another life has been taken, and the executed person's family, too, is desperately asking why nothing was done earlier. . . .

The death penalty is not the answer to the problem of violence committed by persons with severe mental illness. Society's "evolving standards of decency" render the death penalty an inappropriate and disproportionate response to such crimes, as the recent trend in U.S. Supreme Court rulings shows. Moreover, as the testimony of victims' families and families of offenders so vividly demonstrates, executions do not address the central concerns engendered by their incomparable losses. As a society, we owe it to them to do better.

> "A perpetrator should go unpunished ... only if he is found to be completely divorced from reality by diagnosticians from both sides, a far cry from today's insanity defense."

Many People with Mental Illness Should Not Be Exempt from the Death Penalty

Sam Vaknin

Sam Vaknin runs a website about narcissistic personality disorder, and he is the author of Malignant Self-Love: Narcissism Revisited. *In the following viewpoint, Vaknin argues that the insanity defense often is used by criminals as a loophole instead of by truly mentally ill people who have committed a crime. According to Vaknin, the legal system's tests to determine whether a person can be considered mentally ill under the law are often viewed by mental health professionals as subjective, biased, and flawed. Vaknin argues that the only true test of insanity is the reality test: Is the defendant's perception or understanding of reality truly impaired? As someone's perception and understanding of reality can coexist with severe mental illness, Vaknin states that mentally ill suspects should be held criminally responsible if they pass the reality test.*

Sam Vaknin, author of *Malignant Self-Love: Narcissism Revisited* (www.narcissistic-abuse.com). Reproduced by permission.

As you read, consider the following questions:

1. According to the viewpoint, what is diminished capacity?

2. Who does Vaknin cite as an example of a psychopath whose reality was subverted by intense bouts of psychosis?

3. To how many years was serial killer Jeffrey Dahmer sentenced, according to Vaknin?

Levi Aron, who has confessed to kidnapping, murdering and dismembering 8-year-old Leiby Kletzky in Brooklyn last month [July 2011] in a crime that horrified the entire city, has one last resort: to claim that he was insane when he committed the crime.

Having just been found competent enough to eventually stand trial in Brooklyn Supreme Court, Aron and his lawyers will likely now point to a history of "psychiatric disorders," including hearing voices, in an attempt to plead NGRI ("not guilty by reason of insanity"). Yesterday, the Associated Press obtained the report of an evaluation that showed Aron to have an "apathetic" mood—as well as a schizophrenic sister, now deceased.

The insanity defense in criminal trials is nothing new. The Babylonian Talmud had this to say some 1,500 years ago: "It is an ill thing to knock against a deaf-mute, an imbecile or a minor. He that wounds them is culpable, but if they wound him they are not culpable."

The Insanity Defense Does Not Reflect Modern Medical Science

But even the Talmudic rabbis would have been baffled by the modern version of the insanity defense, which has become less about compassion for the mentally ill than a loophole for criminals to escape through.

To start with, no one seems to be able to define "insanity" unequivocally. Insanity in a courtroom is not the same as the colloquial expression (i.e., "he is nuts"). To add to the confusion, it is equally distinct from the way psychiatrists use the term—which, in fact, they rarely do.

Indeed, when it comes to the antiquated insanity defense, the legal profession is completely at odds with modern psychiatry, which recognizes that "insanity" is an inaccurate term to use in describing an incredibly wide spectrum of mental states, not all of which should automatically get a criminal off the judicial hook.

Only Those Separated from Reality Are Truly Insane

The legal system applies three tests to determine whether a suspect should be held not responsible for his or her actions:

- Diminished capacity. Can the suspect tell right from wrong? Does he or she lack substantial capacity to "know and appreciate" the criminality or wrongfulness of the alleged conduct?

- Criminal intent. Did the suspect intend to act in the way that he or she did?

- Irresistible impulse. Was the suspect unable to control his or her behavior?

But many mental health scholars today regard these broad "tests" as subjective, biased and even ludicrous. What matters is whether the defendant's perception or understanding of reality is impaired. This so-called "reality test" is the only true measure of "insanity," critics say.

A perpetrator should go unpunished—and be hospitalized instead—only if he is found to be completely divorced from reality by diagnosticians from both sides, a far cry from today's insanity defense.

But the rigorous criterion of a reality test applies only to psychopaths such as Tucson shooter Jared Lee Loughner [who was charged with killing six people and wounding fourteen others, including US Representative Gabrielle Giffords, on January 8, 2011] whose reality was subverted by apparently intense bouts of psychosis (delusions, hearing voices, etc.). In these extreme instances, a criminal may be so thoroughly unaware of reality that his or her mental state really does deserve courtroom consideration.

All others should be deemed both sane and culpable for all intents and purposes, insist most psychiatrists.

Moreover, a perception and understanding of reality can coexist even with the severest forms of mental illness. Even when a suspect is deemed mentally ill, as long as he or she passes the reality test, that suspect should be held criminally responsible.

Mental Impairment Does Not Equal Insanity

The serial killer Jeffrey Dahmer, accused of killing 17 young men and boys, pleaded NGRI in 1992. Despite obvious mental health troubles, however, the jury rightly found that he was responsible for his actions and sentenced him to more than 900 years in prison.

Consider, also, the cases of the Norway shooter, Anders Behring Breivik [who confessed to bombing government buildings in Oslo, killing eight people, and then killing sixty-nine more people—most teenagers—at a camp on the island of Utaya on July 22, 2011], or Unabomber Ted Kaczynski [a former mathematics professor who was convicted of perpetrating a nearly twenty-year-long mail bombing campaign that killed three people and injured twenty-three others]: Both have coherent worldviews, a consistent internal logic and highly complex ethical codes. Their philosophy may be repellent or outlandish, but that alone does not make them insane.

Breivik, for instance, is not delusional. Yet his lawyer is seriously considering using the insanity defense.

This is not to say that a defendant's mental state at the time of the crime is irrelevant: He or she may have held mistaken (even delusional) beliefs or may have misread the situation, may have been misinformed, may have been under the influence of mind-altering drugs, may have lacked criminal intent, may have been unable to tell right from wrong or to control his or her urges.

A troubled mental state can be accounted for during the sentencing, but the all-purpose insanity defense is an outdated tactic that poorly serves justice and science alike.

Periodical and Internet Sources Bibliography

The following articles have been selected to supplement the diverse views presented in this chapter.

American Civil Liberties Union	"DNA Testing and the Death Penalty," October 3, 2011. www.aclu.org.
American Civil Liberties Union	"Mental Illness and the Death Penalty," May 5, 2009. www.aclu.org.
Mary Kate Cary	"The Conservative Case Against the Death Penalty: Exonerations and Cost Outweigh the Benefits of Capital Punishment," *U.S. News & World Report*, March 30, 2011.
Andrew Cohen	"Another Death Row Debacle: The Case Against Thomas Arthur," *Atlantic*, February 27, 2012.
Joel Cohen	"When a Client Slips Between the Cracks," Law.com, March 19, 2012.
Brandon Garrett	"Learning What We Can from DNA," *Cato Unbound*, March 5, 2012. www.cato-unbound.org.
New York Times	"A Grievous Wrong," September 20, 2011.
New York Times	"An Intolerable Burden of Proof," November 29, 2011.
Mike Thomas	"When Will State Stop Arbitrary Death-Penalty Decisions?," *Orlando Sentinel*, September 7, 2011.
David Zucchino	"North Carolina Judge Vacates Death Penalty Under Racial Justice Law," *Los Angeles Times*, April 20, 2012.

CHAPTER 4

Should the Death Penalty Be Abolished or Reformed?

Chapter Preface

On March 9, 2011, Governor Pat Quinn signed a bill that abolished the death penalty in the state of Illinois, making it the sixteenth state to do so. At the same time, he also commuted the sentences of fifteen death row prisoners to life in prison.

At the time Quinn signed the bill, it had been more than a decade since the last execution had taken place in the state. In 2000 the then governor George Ryan ordered a moratorium on executions, fearing that flaws in the state's death penalty system might lead to the execution of innocent people. Ryan—who had previously favored the death penalty—changed his mind when he began to see an increasing number of death row exonerations throughout the Illinois court system.

By the time he signed the 2011 bill, Governor Quinn had reached the same conclusion. "I have concluded that our system of imposing the death penalty is inherently flawed," Quinn wrote in a statement after signing the bill. "Since our experience has shown that there is no way to design a perfect death penalty system, free from the numerous flaws that can lead to wrongful convictions or discriminatory treatment, I have concluded that the proper course of action is to abolish it."

In addition to the fear of putting innocent people to death, Quinn also cited several other reasons for his decision. "I have found no credible evidence that the death penalty has a deterrent effect on the crime of murder and that the enormous sums expended by the state in maintaining a death penalty system would be better spent on preventing crime and assisting victims' families in overcoming their pain and grief," he said.

As of mid-2012, thirty-three states still allowed for the death penalty. Connecticut became the seventeenth state to abolish the death penalty in April 2012, and Kentucky, Maryland, and several other states have introduced bills to do the same. A coalition in California called Tax Payers for Justice collected more than 750,000 signatures in an attempt to place a death penalty repeal initiative on the November 2012 ballot. The political and public discourse on the death penalty has continued to increase in other states as well, with capital punishment increasingly included as a topic during political debates and campaign speeches.

Though some advocate stopping executions until the death penalty is fixed, others contend that the system is too flawed to be reformed and should be abandoned. Those in favor of abolishing the death penalty often point to the number of death row exonerations—138 since 1973—as an indication that the system risks putting innocent people to death. Many cash-strapped states also cite the exorbitantly high cost of death penalty cases—sometimes as high as $3 million—as one of the main reasons to eliminate capital punishment as a viable alternative for society's worst criminals.

Despite this apparent shift in the tide of public opinion, there are those who contend that abolishing the death penalty is a bad idea. Kent Scheidegger, legal director for the pro–death penalty Criminal Justice Legal Foundation, has said in media reports that the push to end the death penalty is "unfortunate because there are going to be cases where the crime really cries out for the death penalty, and it won't be available. There are times when life in prison without parole is just not a sufficient punishment."

In the following chapter, writers of each of the viewpoints explore whether the death penalty system should be reformed or abolished. While some argue that reform is possible, others contend it is irreparably flawed and broken. Instead of the death penalty, some propose life in prison without parole as an option that appears to be less costly. Proponents of life in prison without parole also say that the punishment eliminates the possibility of wrongfully executing an innocent person.

| "The practice and support for capital punishment is corrosive; . . . I believe we should be better than what we are in our weakest moments."

Death Penalty Is Dead Wrong: It's Time to Outlaw Capital Punishment in America—Completely

Mario M. Cuomo

Mario M. Cuomo is the former governor of New York. In the following viewpoint, he argues that the death penalty is wrong on several different levels and that it is an ineffective form of punishment. In addition, Cuomo states that capital punishment is a misuse of power and gives in to humanity's darkest impulses. In making his case against the death penalty, Cuomo provides anecdotal evidence suggesting that life in prison without parole is a more effective deterrent to crime than capital punishment. In addition, Cuomo asserts, law enforcement efforts must be improved to increase public safety and deal effectively with offenders.

As you read, consider the following questions:

1. What does Cuomo say was an "abomination"?

2. What state does Cuomo say holds the record for the largest number of innocents put to death?

3. What is millions of dollars less expensive than the death penalty, according to Cuomo?

I have studied the death penalty for more than half my life-time. I have debated it hundreds of times. I have heard all the arguments, analyzed all the evidence I could find, measured public opinion when it was opposed to the practice, when it was indifferent and when it was passionately in favor. Always I have concluded the death penalty is wrong because it lowers us all; it is a surrender to the worst that is in us; it uses a power—the official power to kill by execution—that has never elevated a society, never brought back a life, never inspired anything but hate.

And it has killed many innocent people.

This is a serious moral problem for every U.S. governor who presides over executions—whether in Georgia, Texas or even, theoretically, New York. All states should do as the bold few have done and officially outlaw this form of punishment.

For 12 years as governor, I prevented the death penalty from becoming law in New York by my vetoes. But for all that time, there was a disconcertingly strong preference for the death penalty in the general public.

New York returned to the death penalty shortly after I was defeated by a Republican candidate; the state's highest court has effectively prevented the law from being applied—but New York continues to have the law on its books with no signs of a movement to remove it.

That law is a stain on our conscience. The 46 executions in the United States in 2008 were, I believe, an abomination.

People have a right to demand a civilized level of law and peace. They have a right to expect it and when at times it appears to them that a murder has been particularly egregious, it is not surprising that the public anger is great and demands some psychic satisfaction.

I understand that. I have felt the anger myself, more than once. Like too many other citizens, I know what it is to be violated and even to have one's closest family violated through despicable criminal behavior. Even today, I tremble at the thought of how I might react to a killer who took the life of someone in my own family. I know that I might not be able to suppress my anger or put down a desire for revenge, but I also know this society should strive for something better than what it feels at its weakest moments.

There is absolutely no good reason to believe that using death as a punishment today is any better an answer now than it was in the past—when New York State had it, used it, regretted it and discarded it.

Experts throughout the nation have come out strongly against the death penalty after hundreds of years of lawyers' cumulative experiences and studies revealed that the death penalty is ineffective as a deterrent.

Some of history's most notorious murders occurred in the face of existing death penalty statutes.

Psychiatrists will tell you there is reason to believe that some madmen—for example, Ted Bundy—may even be tempted to murder because of a perverse desire to challenge the ultimate penalty.

It is also unfairly applied.

Notwithstanding the executions of mass killers like Timothy McVeigh, capital punishment appears to threaten white drug dealers, white rapists and white killers less frequently than those of other races. Of the last 18 people in New York State to be executed (ending in 1963), 13 were black and one

---

Life in Prison Is Preferred over the Death Penalty

"Which of the following statements do you agree with more? The penalty for first-degree murder should be the death penalty; or the penalty for first-degree murder should be life imprisonment with absolutely no possibility of parole."

	All Adults	Party			Likely Voters
		Dem	Rep	Ind	
Death penalty	39%	34%	60%	40%	45%
Life imprisonment with absolutely no possibility of parole	54	59	35	56	50
Don't know	7	7	5	4	5

TAKEN FROM: Mark Baldassare, Dean Bonner, Sonja Petek, and Jui Shrestha, *PPIC Statewide Survey: Californians and Their Government,* Public Policy Institute of California, September 2011.

---

was Hispanic. That racial makeup seems an extraordinary improbability for a system operating with any kind of objectivity and consistency.

Because death penalty proponents have no other way to defend this policy, they cling unabashedly to the blunt simplicity of the ancient impulse that has always spurred the call for death: the desire for revenge. That was the bottom line of many debates on the floor of the state senate and assembly, to which I listened with great care during my tenure as governor. It came down to "an eye for an eye, tooth for a tooth."

If we adopted this maxim, where would it end? "You kill my son; I kill yours." "You rape my daughter; I rape yours." "You mutilate my body; I mutilate yours." And we would pursue this course, despite the lack of any reason to believe it will protect us even if it is clear that occasionally the victim of our official barbarism will be innocent.

It is believed that at least 23 people were wrongfully executed in the United States during the twentieth century. Twenty-three innocent people killed by the official workings of the state, but it is not called murder.

According to the Innocence Project, 17 people have been proven innocent—exonerated by DNA testing—after serving time on death row. These people were convicted in 11 different states. They served a combined 209 years in prison. And government was prepared to end their lives.

Tragically, New York holds the record for the greatest number of innocents put to death over the years. According to some, New York leads all states with at least six (perhaps more) wrongful executions since 1905.

Yet proponents of the death penalty continue to assume that the criminal justice system will not make a mistake, or they simply don't care. As was shown by the recent Troy Davis execution in Georgia, where shaky witness testimony and a lack of physical evidence were considered insufficient to create "reasonable doubt," too many people seem unconcerned about the overly ambitious prosecutor, the sloppy detective, the incompetent defense counsel, the witness with an ax to grind, the judge who keeps courthouse conviction box scores.

But these imperfections—as well as the horrible and irreversible injustice they can produce—are inevitable. In this country, a defendant is convicted on proof beyond a reasonable doubt—not proof that can be known with absolute certainty. There's no such thing as absolute certainty in our law.

We need to continue to do the things that will control crime by making the apprehension and punishment of criminals more effective and more precise. We need adequate police and prisons and alternatives to incarceration. We should also have a tough, effective punishment for deliberate murder. There is a punishment that is much better than the death penalty: one that juries will not be reluctant to impose; one that is so menacing to a potential killer, that it could actually deter; one that does not require us to be infallible so as to avoid taking an innocent life; and one that does not require us to stoop to the level of the killers.

There is a penalty that is—for those who insist on measuring this question in terms of financial cost—millions of dollars less expensive than the death penalty: true life imprisonment, with no possibility of parole under any circumstances.

True life imprisonment is a more effective deterrent than capital punishment. To most inmates, the thought of living a whole lifetime behind bars only to die in a cell is worse than the quick, final termination of the electric chair or lethal injection.

I've heard this sentiment personally at least three times in my life. The second time it came from a man on the way to his execution in Oklahoma. He was serving a life sentence for murder in New York at the same time that Oklahoma was eager to take him from New York so they could execute him for a murder he had committed in Oklahoma. I refused to release him so that he could be executed in Oklahoma, but then the governor who replaced me in 1995 was able to get New York to adopt the death penalty—and to prove New York really approved of death as a punishment, he released the inmate from prison and sent him to Oklahoma, where he was promptly executed.

On the night before he died, he left a note that was published in the *New York Post* that said, "Tell Governor Cuomo I would rather be executed than to serve life behind bars."

Because the death penalty was so popular during the time I served as governor, I was often asked why I spoke out so forcefully against it although the voters very much favored it. I tried to explain that I pushed this issue into the center of public dialogue because I believed the stakes went far beyond the death penalty itself. Capital punishment raises important questions about how, as a society, we view human beings. I believed as governor, and I still believe, that the practice and support for capital punishment is corrosive; that it is bad for a democratic citizenry and that it had to be objected to, and so I did then and I do now and will continue to for as long as it and I exist, because I believe we should be better than what we are in our weakest moments.

> *"The death penalty is an awesome punishment. It should be applied sparingly to the most egregious and shocking crimes committed by the most unrepentant and callous offenders."*

The Death Penalty Should Not Be Abolished

Bruce Fein

Bruce Fein is an author and constitutional law expert who served as associate deputy attorney during President Ronald Reagan's administration. In the following viewpoint, Fein asserts that arguments presented by death penalty abolitionists are unpersuasive and do not stand up to close scrutiny. Furthermore, Fein says that some crimes are so morally abhorrent and despicable that only the death penalty is adequate punishment for them. Despite his support for retaining the death penalty, however, Fein states that while the death penalty is necessary, it should be used infrequently, for only crimes involving the most heinous actions and offenders. Fein argues that those who contend that the government should not be involved in actions causing death ignore the government's role in sending soldiers to war, where many of them are killed.

As you read, consider the following questions:

1. According to Fein, what did the US Supreme Court decide in *McCleskey v. Kemp*?

2. How does the death penalty honor human dignity, according to Fein?

3. According to Fein, what are two things worth killing for?

Death penalty abolitionists are unpersuasive. Whoever shed a tear over the trial and execution of Adolf Eichmann by Israel for his unspeakable complicity in the Holocaust? Ditto for Japanese archvillain Hideki Tojo for Pearl Harbor, the Rape of Nanking, the Bataan Death March, and gruesome bacteriological experimentation on U.S. prisoners of war. Or who would balk at capital punishment for an American who lethally poisoned hundreds of thousands by resorting to biological or chemical contamination of the nation's water supplies?

Some crimes betray a reptilian immorality and beastliness that only the supreme penalty of death can adequately answer. Anything less would trivialize the preciousness of humanity. This proposition cannot be proven with the certitude of euclidean geometry. It is not a matter of doing sums. Instead, the axiom rests on intuition, instinct, and a moral sensitivity that palpitates in the hearts of the vast majority of mankind. Indeed, could any capital punishment abolitionist stand at the chilling Auschwitz cemetery; look in the eyes of a Holocaust survivor whose mother, father, and siblings had died in [Adolf] Hitler's cyanide chambers; and preach that the death penalty for Der Fuehrer would have been too draconian for the genocide of six million? The death penalty is not unique in summoning unprovable moral assertions in its defense. The criminal law is dominated by common moral hunches and sentiments that elude empirical proof. Theft is punished, although a right to private property is debatable. [French philosopher Pierre-Joseph] Proudhon insisted that "property is theft," whereas [German philosopher Jean-Jacques] Rousseau sermonized, "The first man who, having fenced in a piece of land, said, 'This is mine,' and found people naive enough to believe him, that man was the true founder of civil society."

The crimes of rape, torture, treason, kidnapping, murder, larceny, and perjury pivot on a moral code that escapes apodictic [absolute] proof by expert testimony or otherwise. But communities would plunge into anarch—a state of nature where life is poor, brutish, nasty, and short, according to [English philosopher Thomas] Hobbes—if they could not act on moral assumptions less certain than that the sun will rise in the east and set in the west.

Arguments Against the Death Penalty Do Not Stand Up to Scrutiny

Abolitionists may contend that the death penalty is inherently immoral because governments should never take human life, no matter what the provocation. But that is an article of faith, not of fact, just like the opposite position held by abolitionist detractors, including myself. All of the instrumental or complementary reasons chorused by anti–death penalty supporters do not withstand scrutiny.

Capital punishment is not invariably degrading or humiliating. A nontrivial number of death penalty inmates covet their punishments and have thwarted legal efforts to challenge their sentences. To believe they would invite degradation or humiliation is to deny human nature. Death penalty crimes are not uniformly vulnerable to error in proving guilt. Tens of millions witnessed Jack Ruby's assassination of Lee Harvey Oswald on television, and companion gruesome murders have been equally beyond dispute. It might be said that since capital punishment is irrevocable, an additional safeguard against convicting the innocent is justified: namely, proof beyond a slight doubt, not just beyond a reasonable doubt. But that contention militates in favor of reform, not abolition.

Abolitionists might deplore the inferior legal talents and assiduity of defense counsel for indigents in capital cases. The reproach, however, argues in favor of upgrading indigent defense, a project under way in several states—Illinois and Texas are prime examples—and the U.S. Congress. It does not demonstrate that capital punishment is intrinsically wrong or barbaric.

It has been urged that the death penalty disproportionately impacts minorities. Under the U.S. Supreme Court's 1986 decision in *Batson v. Kentucky*, 476 U.S. 79 (1986), however, prospective jurors may not be struck because of race, and intentional discrimination in selecting death penalty candidates by prosecutors would violate the Fourteenth Amendment. The next year, in *McCleskey v. Kemp*, 481 U.S. 279 (1987), the court denied that capital punishment statistics assembled in Georgia proved that minority defendants were treated more harshly because of race than their white counterparts in capital cases. In any event, the remedy for a racially discriminatory death penalty is to end the racism, not the punishment.

Contrary to abolitionist arguments, evolving standards of decency do not condemn capital punishment. In the United States, a plurality of Americans opposed the death penalty in 1966. After the crime rate spiraled, that sentiment galloped into a commanding majority for capital punishment. In the wake of the Supreme Court's 1972 decision in *Furman v. Georgia*, 408 U.S. 238 (1972), nullifying all capital punishment laws as then applied without certain procedural safeguards, a decisive majority of thirty-eight state legislatures responded with revamped death penalty statutes that channeled sentencing discretion. Sister federal death penalty statutes were also enacted. In other words, evolving moral standards in the United States have not been a one-way street when capital punishment has been the issue; the standards have shifted both in favor of and against the death penalty, not remained fixed like the North Star. The Philippines similarly ended the death penalty under President Cory Aquino but then opted for restoration because of a meteoric jump in crime, including death for Imelda Marcos–like corruption.[1] Currently, the Philippines has a moratorium on executions in place.

At present, when crime rates are tumbling, a dwindling majority of Americans support the death penalty. That majority might further fall to a minority. But history shows that death penalty proponents could again capture the majority viewpoint. In any event, the evolving-standards-of-decency argument works more against than in support of abolitionists.

Associate Justice William Brennan insisted in his concurring opinion in *Furman* that the death penalty degrades human dignity because it implicates the state in the deliberate extinguishment of human life. But the *ipse dixit* [Latin phrase, meaning "he himself said it"] is unconvincing. The death penalty honors human dignity by treating the defendant as a free moral actor able to control his own destiny for good or for ill; it does not treat him as an animal with no moral sense, and thus subject even to butchery to satiate human gluttony. Moreover, capital punishment celebrates the dignity of the humans whose lives were ended by the defendant's predation. Nothing less would adequately give expression to the sacredness of innocent life.

The Death Penalty Is No Different than Sending Soldiers into Combat

Conscription and war, like the death penalty, also involve government action that knowingly will precipitate the extinguishment of human life. And the dead conscripts, unlike a capital criminal, will be free of any legal or moral guilt. Indeed, they

---

1. Imelda Marcos is a Filipina politician known for her extravagant lifestyle as the wife of former president Ferdinand Marcos.

may deserve and enjoy commemoration and burial on hallowed ground, like Civil War Union soldiers who gave that last full measure of devotion for a new birth of freedom.

Unlike with the death penalty, of course, the government does not know in advance the identities of its war casualties. But it customarily knows many of its citizens will perish, whether at Gettysburg, Iwo Jima, or the Battle of the Bulge. If government participation in the extinguishment of human life is inherently an immoral degradation of human dignity, then pacifism must also be advocated. That means playing spectator to an impending Holocaust, a Pol Pot, or Rwandan genocide; a nuclear, biological, or chemical attack on citizens of the United States; or any other evil of nauseating proportions. Indeed, absolute pacifism would require the U.S. government to forgo conscription and war to defend our fundamental human rights and liberties from extinction by a foreign aggressor. But such pusillanimity [cowardliness] and consignment of hundreds of millions to the chains of despotism to avoid implication in the killing of humans seems itself a disgusting affront to human dignity. Some things are worth killing for, including a free mind and a free country. That is why our war heroes who rained death on the enemy are lionized, not despised.

The death penalty is first cousin to conscription and war. In both cases, the government exercises coercion and undertakes action that it knows will end human life. In the former, the justification is retribution commensurate with the sacredness of the lives taken by the defendants in cold blood. In the latter, the government sacrifices the lives of its citizens to protect our constitutional dispensation from domestic or foreign enemies or for related reasons of urgent national security.

In sum, the abolitionist proposition that government implication in the extinguishment of human life is, simpliciter, an unmitigated moral evil that should never be tolerated is untenable unless the anti–death penalty crusaders also embrace absolute pacifism. But the latter, history has proved (think of Munich in 1938)[2] gives birth to wickedness and horrors on a scale shocking to any person with a crumb of humanity. Abolitionists have assembled no convincing moral argument to distinguish the death penalty for retribution from conscription and war in the name of human freedom and dignity. Yet they seem to accept the latter while savaging the former.

The Death Penalty Should Be Applied Sparingly

Justice Thurgood Marshall, in his *Furman* concurrence, staunchly maintained that the death penalty is "morally unacceptable to the people of the United States at this time in their history." That assertion, however, as [English philosopher Jeremy] Bentham said of the common law, is nonsense on stilts. Justice Marshall conceded that the majority, if polled, would favor capital punishment. . . . If Americans attended the likes of Harvard Law School to master death penalty gospel, like King Arthur's tutelage by Merlin, then they would be convinced of capital punishment's iniquity. Furthermore, said the jurist: "I cannot believe that at this stage in our history, the American people would ever knowingly support purposeless vengeance [i.e., retribution]. Thus, I believe that the great mass of citizens would conclude on the basis of the material already considered that the death penalty is immoral, and therefore unconstitutional."

Marshall's idea that the law should echo what citizens would believe if properly indoctrinated by an elite—an earmark of tyranny from time immemorial—is too outlandish to need refutation among a people who celebrate government of the people, by the people, and for the people. It belongs in George Orwell's *1984*.

2. Under the so-called Munich Agreement in 1938, Czechoslovakia was forced to concede territory to Nazi Germany in exchange for not starting a war in Europe.

The death penalty is an awesome punishment. It should be applied sparingly to the most egregious and shocking crimes committed by the most unrepentant and callous offenders. A few procedural safeguards, as noted, should be added to ensure against convicting the innocent. But the punishment itself should be retained as a community affirmation that to treasure life occasionally necessitates the extinguishment of the lives of its most abominable enemies.

> *"Opponents of the death penalty believe that no one deserves to be executed. . . . So they spend all of their energy cherry-picking cases, gumming up the legal system, and talking about 'uncertainty.'"*

Why Death-Penalty Opponents Can't Win

Jonah Goldberg

Jonah Goldberg is an award-winning journalist and both the founding editor and editor at large for the National Review Online. *In the following viewpoint, Goldberg discredits death penalty opponents' arguments, because, he asserts, they are selective about the cases they highlight in their public campaigns. He also points out that death penalty abolitionists base much of their opposition on the idea that there is no such thing as absolute certainty about guilt or innocence in the current system. Goldberg refutes this argument and contends that just because some defendants or convicts are found to be not guilty does not mean that others who are guilty should not be punished. He concludes that because death penalty opponents cannot argue effectively against execution when there is no doubt about the accused's guilt, they will never be successful in abolishing the practice.*

As you read, consider the following questions:

1. According to Goldberg, why did Lawrence Russell Brewer claim he was innocent?

2. How many people did Timothy McVeigh admit to killing, according to the viewpoint?

3. Why, according to Goldberg, are death penalty opponents less eager to debate cases in which DNA evidence confirms criminals' guilt?

On Wednesday, two men were lawfully executed. Both insisted they were innocent. If you've been watching the news or following Kim Kardashian's tweets, you've likely heard of one of these men, Troy Davis.

The other death-penalty "victim," Lawrence Russell Brewer, was until this week the more significant convicted murderer. Brewer was one of the racist goons who infamously tied James Byrd to the back of their truck and dragged him to death in Texas.

The case became a touchstone in the 2000 presidential race because then Texas governor George W. Bush had refused to sign a "hate crimes" law. The NAACP ran a reprehensible ad during the presidential election trying to insinuate that Bush somehow shared responsibility for the act.

Regardless, Brewer claimed that he was "innocent" because one of his buddies had cut Byrd's throat before they dragged his body around. Forensic evidence directly contradicted this.

Brewer's own statements didn't help either. Such as, "As far as any regrets, no, I have no regrets. . . . I'd do it all over again, to tell you the truth."

Brewer, festooned with tattoos depicting KKK symbols and burning crosses, was "not a sympathetic person" in the words of Gloria Rubac of the Texas Death Penalty Abolition Movement.

Which is why we didn't hear much about him this week. Instead, we heard a great deal about Davis. Many people insist Davis was innocent or that there was "too much doubt" about his guilt to proceed with the execution. Many judges and public officials disagreed, including all nine members of the Supreme Court, who briefly stayed the execution Wednesday night, only to let it proceed hours later.

There are many sincere and decent people—on both sides of the ideological spectrum—who are opposed to the death penalty. I consider it an honorable position, even though I disagree with it. I am 100 percent in favor of lawfully executing people who deserve the death penalty and 100 percent opposed to killing people who do not deserve it.

When I say that, many death-penalty opponents angrily respond that I'm missing the point. You can never be certain! Troy Davis proves that!

But he proves no such thing. At best, his case proves that you can't be certain about Davis. You most certainly can be certain about other murderers. If the horrible happens and we learn that Davis really was not guilty, that will be a heart-wrenching revelation. It will cast a negative light on the death penalty, on the Georgia criminal-justice system, and on America.

But you know what it won't do? It won't render Lawrence Russell Brewer one iota less guilty or less deserving of the death penalty. Opponents of capital punishment are extremely selective about the cases they make into public crusades. Strategically, that's smart; you don't want to lead your argument with "unsympathetic persons." But logically, it's problematic. There is no transitive property that renders one heinous murderer less deserving of punishment simply because some other person was exonerated of murder.

Timothy McVeigh killed 168 people including 19 children. He admitted it. How does doubt in Troy Davis's case make McVeigh less deserving of death?

We hear so much about the innocent people who've gotten off death row—thank God—because of new DNA techniques. We hear very little about the criminals who've had their guilt confirmed by the same techniques (or who've declined DNA testing because they know it will remove all doubt). Death-penalty opponents are less eager to debate such cases because they want to delegitimize "the system."

And to be fair, I think this logic cuts against one of the death penalty's greatest rationalizations as well: deterrence. I do believe there's a deterrence effect from the death penalty. But I don't think that's anything more than an ancillary benefit of capital punishment. It's unjust to kill a person simply to send a message to other people who've yet to commit a crime. It is just to execute a person who deserves to be executed.

Opponents of the death penalty believe that no one deserves to be executed. Again, it's an honorable position, but a difficult one to defend politically in a country where the death penalty is popular. So they spend all of their energy cherry-picking cases, gumming up the legal system, and talking about "uncertainty."

That's fine. But until they can explain why we shouldn't have a death penalty when uncertainty isn't an issue—i.e., why McVeigh and Brewer should live—they'll never win the real argument.

> *"Until the day comes when we are able to guarantee that our system will never put innocent men and women to death, we can't continue to use a form of punishment that is irreversible."*

Executions Should Stop Until the Capital Punishment Process Is Reformed

Michael Hall

Michael Hall is an award-winning writer for Texas Monthly *and a contributor to other publications, including the* New York Times. *In the following viewpoint, Hall presents examples of how a flawed death penalty system, prosecutorial misconduct, unreliable scientific evidence, and human error have resulted in wrongful convictions and innocents sitting on death row in Texas. Hall argues that until officials can guarantee that the system is fixed and that no innocent people will be put to death, there needs to be a ban on the death penalty in that state. To fix the system, Hall suggests, law enforcement must rely only upon proven forensic science, and district attorneys must be motivated to achieve just results rather than simply convictions. Nevertheless, Hall concludes, because human error is unavoidable, the capital punishment system can never be free of error.*

As you read, consider the following questions:

1. What type of forensic analysis was used to convict Claude Jones and Michael Blair, according to Hall?

2. What did Robert Carter tell the district attorney the night before he was to testify at Anthony Graves's trial, according to Hall?

3. What, according to Hall, did Keith Pikett claim his bloodhounds could do?

It's time to halt executions in Texas. The flaws in our death penalty system have become too obvious to ignore any longer. Five times in the past seven years we've learned about a person wrongly convicted and taken off death row or a person convicted on bogus forensic science—and executed. It's clear: Until the day comes when we are able to guarantee that our system will never put innocent men and women to death, we can't continue to use a form of punishment that is irreversible. It's time for Texas to put a moratorium on capital punishment.

This is a law-and-order state, and most citizens support executing murderers. But what about executing people who haven't done anything wrong? The new legislature that convenes this month [in January 2011] is the most conservative in history, with 22 freshman lawmakers, many of them Tea Party–inspired folks who promised their constituents that they were going to Austin [the capital of Texas] to grapple with the tyranny of the government. On the campaign trail, these men and women railed against the ineptitude and interference of government in general, about the way the state tramples on the lives of its citizens. "Don't tread on me!" they cried. Fine, then. Let's look at recent history, which has offered some appalling examples of the state's treading all over its citizens.

Recent Death Penalty Cases Highlight the Failings of the System

In the summer of 2008, Michael Blair, who was convicted of a Plano murder in 1994 based on hair-comparison analysis, was taken off death row following a series of DNA tests that showed he was not guilty of the crime. One year later, a nationwide controversy erupted over the case of Cameron Todd Willingham, a Corsicana man who was convicted in 1992 and executed twelve years later for setting a fire that killed his children. No fewer than seven subsequent reports revealed that Willingham's conviction was based on forensic science that amounted to little more than folklore. The case bore a striking similarity to that of Ernest Willis, who spent seventeen years on death row for setting a deadly house fire in Iraan [Texas] before he was exonerated and set free in 2004. This past November, the Innocence Project and the *Texas Observer* announced the results of an investigation into the case of Claude Jones, who was convicted of murdering a liquor store owner in 1989 and executed in 2000. Like Blair, Jones had been convicted largely based on the analysis of hair—in Jones's case a single strand found at the crime scene. But DNA testing on the hair showed that it wasn't his at all.

Finally there's the case of Anthony Graves, which we wrote about in tremendous detail back in October and have followed up on this month. Graves was convicted of a brutal 1992 murder and sentenced to death. There was no evidence to connect him to the crime, no plausible motive, and the only person who could place him at the scene was the crime's actual perpetrator, Robert Carter, who was executed in 2000 and who had repeatedly recanted his testimony and proclaimed Graves's innocence. Nonetheless, Graves spent eighteen years behind bars—twelve of them on death row—and was about to face a retrial next month when Burleson County district attorney [DA] Bill Parham abruptly set him free. To summarize: Agents of the state grabbed a completely innocent man out of his mother's apartment, prosecuted him for capital murder, and kept him locked away for almost two decades.

What can we learn from Graves's ordeal? Governor Rick Perry, campaigning in Lubbock two days later, was asked by a reporter about the case. "I think we have a justice system that is working, and he's a good example," Perry said. "I think our system works well; it goes through many layers of observation and appeal, et cetera. So I think our system is working."

In fact, the Graves case proves the exact opposite. Graves was failed every step of the way by the system—or, to be more precise, by imperfect humans working in a flawed system. He, like so many other wrongly convicted death row inmates, had inexperienced trial attorneys who were no match for a powerful prosecutor. He was also failed by the judges on the state appellate courts; the Court of Criminal Appeals, the highest of Perry's fail-safe layers of appeal, turned him down three times.

Mostly, however, Graves was failed by Charles Sebesta, the district attorney in Burleson County at the time of his arrest. State law directs DAs "not to convict, but to see that justice is done." But early on Sebesta and the investigators working the case developed a theory that Carter could not have committed the crime alone, and they settled on Graves as his accomplice. The night before Carter was set to testify at Graves's trial, he told the DA, "I did it all myself, Mr. Sebesta." But nothing was going to keep the DA from winning. After discussing it with Sebesta, Carter testified at trial the next day that Graves was the murderer.

Prosecutor Misconduct Leads to Wrongfully Imprisoned Death Row Inmates

The system that Perry says is working would never have discovered this shocking detail had it not been for an offhand comment that Sebesta made in a Geraldo Rivera documentary in 2000, six years after the DA had sent Graves to death row. On the show, Sebesta let slip that Carter had told him he had

The Criminal Justice System Must Exemplify Fairness and Accuracy

Fairness and accuracy form the foundation of the American criminal justice system. As the Supreme Court of the United States has recognized, these goals are particularly important in cases in which the death penalty is sought. Our system cannot claim to provide due process or protect the innocent unless it offers a fair and accurate system for every person who faces the death penalty.

"Evaluating Fairness and Accuracy in State Death Penalty Systems: The Missouri Death Penalty Assessment Report," American Bar Association, April 2012. www.americanbar.org.

acted alone. That comment was evidence of a conversation that Graves's defense attorneys said Sebesta had never revealed before. Springing into action, Graves's new appellate lawyers got to work writing a federal appeal, which led a federal court to overturn the murder conviction in 2006 and order the state to retry Graves or set him free. But for Sebesta's comment, Graves would almost certainly be dead by now. Does it need to be said that a system reliant on Geraldo Rivera is a system that needs work?

"Charles Sebesta handled this case in a way that would best be described as a criminal justice system's nightmare," special prosecutor Kelly Siegler told reporters after Graves was released. "It's a travesty." But his case is not an aberration. We know of several other Texas death penalty cases where the very qualities we value in our prosecutors—ambition, relentlessness—led them to refuse to be skeptical of shaky witnesses, to refuse to admit error, to push on at all costs. Randall Dale Adams was convicted of killing a Dallas police officer and sent to death row in 1977. He was released in 1989, after his accuser confessed to the crime himself and a higher court stated that the prosecutors had "knowingly used perjured testimony." Kerry Max Cook was convicted of killing a woman in Tyler in 1977. He was released in 1997 and his conviction reversed; the Court of Criminal Appeals found that the state had hidden critical evidence. And then there's Ernest Willis, who was pumped so full of antipsychotic medicine during his trial that he appeared to jurors as a blank-eyed maniac—a fact the prosecutor made great use of at trial.

And these are just the cases we know of. Are there other wrongfully imprisoned people sitting on death row right now whose stories will never come out? Before you answer that question, think about what went into saving Graves. Nicole Casarez, a professor at the University of St. Thomas, in Houston, and a dozen of her students spent thousands of hours poring over the case and interviewing people. Graves also had the benefit of good, experienced lawyers and journalists who worked hard to explain his case. And Graves wasn't the only one with outside help: Just about every single exoneree who has walked off death row has done so in spite of the system, not because of it. The confession that led to Adams's release was propelled by a documentary film; Cook has a New Jersey prison ministry to thank for his freedom; Willis was lucky enough to wind up with a New York lawyer whose firm spent more than $5 million on his case. Without these benefits, Graves, Adams, Cook, Willis—all of whom are innocent men—would likely have been put to death. And, needless to say, the vast majority of the men on death row will never be so lucky as to have a high-priced lawyer or a filmmaker or a posse of journalism students working on their behalf.

System Reforms Are Essential

So what's to be done? First of all, let's admit, finally, that we have a problem. Second, we have to halt all executions: We can't allow a process so flawed to continue doling out the ultimate punishment. Finally, we need to examine the system from top to bottom with a sharp, skeptical eye. Consider forensic science. As late as 2009, investigators from the attorney general's office were trying to work the Graves case using the services of Keith Pikett, a deputy from Fort Bend County who said his bloodhounds could pick the smells of criminals out of scent lineups. Pikett wore out his welcome with law enforcement after sending at least five people to prison for crimes they didn't commit. This didn't happen in the dark ages before DNA. This happened in the past few years.

As the Graves case makes clear, we need to pay attention to the conduct of our district attorneys. They're usually among the most powerful people in any county, and at present there are hardly any criminal or civil penalties for prosecutors who engage in misconduct. We need to create real incentives for our DAs to seek justice instead of convictions. This won't be easy. Sebesta still claims he did nothing wrong—as did the men who prosecuted Adams, Cook, and Willis. They were the good guys fighting the good fight, and if sometimes they got zealous, well, who can blame them? They're only human.

Which brings us to the heart of the problem. Can the criminal justice system, a system conceived and operated by humans, ever be completely free of error? The common theme in the cases of Graves, Willis, Cook, and Adams (and Willingham and Jones) is clear: People make mistakes, and so do the institutions they work for. We know this intuitively. We see it every day, when, say, the postman mistakenly delivers our neighbor's mail or when officials at a football game screw up a call. We can afford these kinds of mistakes. We walk the letter next door. We scream at the TV. But it's different when we're dealing with capital punishment. We can afford the mistaken holding penalty. We can't afford the mistaken death penalty. It's time to halt executions in Texas.

| *"If society's ultimate punishment cannot be applied fairly, it should not be applied at all."*

The Death Penalty Cannot Be Reformed and Should Be Abolished

Richard C. Dieter

Richard C. Dieter is an attorney and executive director of the Death Penalty Information Center. In the following viewpoint, Dieter argues that the death penalty—despite recent reforms and court rulings—still is arbitrary and unfair. Dieter shows that while the death penalty still is in decline across the country, it continues to be imposed in an arbitrary and unjust fashion. Dieter states that attempts to fix the death penalty have failed thus far and that unless the death penalty can be applied fairly, it should not be applied at all.

As you read, consider the following questions:

1. As of 2011 when the viewpoint was written, how many states does Dieter say have abandoned the death penalty since 2007?

Richard C. Dieter, "Struck by Lightning: The Continuing Arbitrariness of the Death Penalty Thirty-Five Years After Its Re-Instatement in 1976," Death Penalty Information Center, July 2011, pp. 3–6, 28–29. Copyright © 2011 by Death Penalty Information Center. All rights reserved. Reproduced by permission.

2. What was the ratio of executions to murders committed in 2010, according to the viewpoint?

3. What percentage of those sentenced to death since 1976 have been executed, according to the author?

The only lengthy, nationwide suspension of the death penalty in U.S. history officially began in 1972 when the U.S. Supreme Court held in *Furman v. Georgia* that the death penalty was being administered in an arbitrary and capricious manner that amounted to cruel and unusual punishment. As in Georgia, the statutes of other states and the federal government provided no guidance to the jury empanelled to decide between sentences of life and death. The death penalty ground to a halt as states formulated revised laws they hoped would win the court's approval.

Executions had stopped in 1967 as lower courts anticipated a high court ruling on the constitutionality of capital punishment. Insights from the civil rights movement of the 1960s led many to believe the death penalty was so linked to the practice of racial discrimination that it would no longer be constitutionally acceptable. When the Supreme Court reviewed the practice of capital punishment, it focused primarily on arbitrariness in its application rather than on racial discrimination. Nevertheless, as Justice William O. Douglas warned in his concurring opinion in *Furman*, the questions of arbitrariness and discrimination are closely linked.

For a pivotal set of justices, the death penalty was unconstitutional because it was "so wantonly and so freakishly imposed." Justice Potter Stewart said the death penalty was "cruel and unusual in the same way that being struck by lightning is cruel and unusual." Justice Byron White echoed that sentiment when he said he could not uphold a punishment where "there is no meaningful basis for distinguishing the few cases in which it is imposed from the many cases in which it is not."

The justices left for another day the question of whether the death penalty itself was constitutional, leaving the door open to the enactment of more limited death penalty statutes that provided detailed guidance for juries. After *Furman*, many states rewrote their death penalty laws and began sentencing people to death—although no executions would be carried out until the court again addressed the issue.

It did so in 1976, approving the new laws of Georgia, Florida and Texas, while rejecting the approach taken by North Carolina and Louisiana, which required all those convicted of certain murders to be sentenced to death, without regard to individual sentencing considerations. The death penalty itself was declared constitutional under the assumption that it fit the rationales of retribution and deterrence. The court said that being sentenced to death would no longer be random because the new statutes sufficiently restricted and guided the decision making of prosecutors, judges, and juries—at least in theory. Whether these new laws would be less arbitrary in practice remained to be seen.

Decades of Experimentation Have Yielded Poor Results

By now thirty-five years have passed, providing ample experience to assess whether this system reliably selects the worst offenders and the most heinous crimes to merit the most severe punishment. This experience also provides an opportunity to judge whether the death penalty's twin rationales—retribution and deterrence—sufficiently justify its continued use, or whether it has devolved into the "pointless and needless extinction of life" forbidden by the Eighth Amendment.

Concerns about the death penalty before the court's approval of new laws in 1976 stemmed not only from the lack of guidance for jurors making crucial choices between life and death sentences. The death penalty was also rarely carried out, giving rise to doubts about its consistent application. In a country with only a handful of executions each year, it was not at all clear that the few executed were the "worst of the worst." Justice [William J.] Brennan [Jr.], concurring with the majority in *Furman*, wrote, "When the punishment of death is inflicted in a trivial number of the cases in which it is legally available, the conclusion is virtually inescapable that it is being inflicted arbitrarily. Indeed, it smacks of little more than a lottery system."

The death penalty is again in decline across the country. The number of death sentences and executions has decreased sharply in the past decade. Since 2007 four states have abandoned the death penalty. Even in the 34 states that retain it [in 2011], an execution is a rare event in all but a handful of states. Less than one in a hundred murders results in a death sentence, and far fewer defendants are executed. Does the one murderer in a hundred who receives a death sentence clearly merit execution more than all, or even most, of the 99 other offenders who remain in prison for life? Or do arbitrary factors continue to determine who lives and who dies under our death penalty laws?

Arbitrariness Is Rampant in the Death Penalty System

The death penalty system in this country is demonstrably highly selective in meting out sentences and executions, and becoming more so. There are approximately 15,000 murders a year; in 2010, there were 46 executions, a ratio of 1 execution for every 326 murders. The number of murders in the U.S. barely changed from 1999 to 2009, but the number of death sentences declined by 60% during that period. Studies of the death penalty in several states since 1976 reveal a system that sweeps broadly through thousands of eligible cases but ends up condemning to death only a small number, with little rational explanation for the disparity.

- In *New Mexico,* during a 28-year span, 211 capital cases were filed. About half the cases resulted in a plea bargain for a sentence less than death. Another half went to trial, and 15 people were sentenced to death. In the end, only one person was executed (after dropping his appeals), and two people were left on death row when the state abolished the death penalty in 2009.

- In *Maryland,* over a 21-year period from 1978 to 1999, 1,227 homicides were identified as death-eligible cases. Prosecutors filed a death notice in 162 cases. Fifty-six cases resulted in a death judgment, although it has become clear the vast majority of those will never be carried out. As of 2011, five defendants have been executed, and only five remain on death row. There have been no executions since 2005.

- In *Washington,* from 1981 to 2006, 254 cases were identified as death eligible. Death notices were filed in 79, and death sentences were imposed in 30. Of the cases that completed the appeals process, 83% were reversed. Four executions took place, with three of the four defendants having waived their remaining appeals.

- In *Kentucky,* from 1979 to 2009, there were 92 death sentences. Of the 50 cases that completed their appeals, 42 sentences (84%) were reversed. Three inmates were executed, including two who waived their appeals.

Patterns in other states are similar. In Oregon, 795 cases were deemed eligible for the death penalty after its reinstatement in 1984; two people have been executed—both "volunteers." Nationally, only about 15% of those sentenced to death since 1976 have been executed. Under the federal death penalty, from a pool of over 2,500 cases submitted by U.S. attorneys, the attorney general has authorized seeking the death penalty in 472 cases; 270 defendants went to trial, resulting in 68 death sentences and three executions to date.

The theory behind winnowing from the many defendants who are eligible for the death penalty down to the few who are executed is that the system is selecting the "worst of the worst" for execution. The Supreme Court recently underscored this theory in a 2008 decision restricting the death penalty: "[C]apital punishment must 'be limited to those offenders who commit "a narrow category of the most serious crimes" and whose extreme culpability makes them "the most deserving of execution.""

However, the notion that tens of thousands of eligible cases are carefully narrowed down to the worst ones does not withstand scrutiny. Many factors determine who is ultimately executed in the U.S.; often the severity of the crime and the culpability of the defendant fade from consideration as other arbitrary factors determine who lives and who dies. . . .

When the death penalty was permitted to go forward in 1976, many distinguished legal scholars warned that the task of creating an objectively fair system for deciding which criminals deserved to die and which should be allowed to live was impossible. A majority of those on the Supreme Court that approved the experiment ultimately concluded the attempt to fix the death penalty had failed.

Thirty-five years later, a strong body of empirical evidence confirms that race, geography, money, politics, and other arbitrary factors exert a powerful influence on determining who is sentenced to death. This is the conclusion not only of experts, but increasingly that of the general public as well. Unfairness ranks near the top of the American public's concerns about the death penalty.

No Rational Reasons for Retaining the Death Penalty Remain

As the use of the death penalty has declined, the rationale for its continuation has disappeared. With defendants already facing life without parole, no one is likely to be deterred by an added punishment that is rarely imposed and even more rarely

"New Jersey ends death penalty," cartoon by Jimmy Margulies, www.PoliticalCartoons .com. Copyright © 2007 by Jimmy Margulies, www.PoliticalCartoons.com. All rights reserved. Reproduced by permission.

carried out many years later, and that is dependent on so many unpredictable factors. Nor does the wish for retribution justify a death penalty that is applied so sporadically. The reality is that those in society generally, and those families of murder victims in particular, who look to an execution to counter a terrible homicide will very likely be disappointed. Very few of those cases result in execution, and those that do are often not the most heinous, but merely the most unlucky, recalling Justice Stewart's comparison in 1972 that receiving the death penalty is like being struck by lightning.

No longer looking only to the Supreme Court to review these issues, some states are choosing to act on their own. Four states in the past four years have abolished the death penalty, bringing the total of states without capital punishment to sixteen [in 2011]. As growing costs and stark unfairness become harder to justify, more states are likely to follow that path.

The post-*Gregg* [*Gregg v. Georgia* (1976)] death penalty in the United States has proven to be a failed experiment. The theory that with proper guidance to juries the death penalty could be administered fairly has not worked in practice. Thirty-five years of experience have taught the futility of trying to fix this system. Many of those who favored the death penalty in the abstract have come to view its practice very differently. They have reached the conclusion that if society's ultimate punishment cannot be applied fairly, it should not be applied at all.

"Death by incarceration is just as final, just as painful, and just as worthy of the careful scrutiny to which we subject traditional capital sentences."

Incarceration for Life Without Parole Could Replace the Death Penalty

Robert Johnson and Sandra McGunigall-Smith

Robert Johnson is a professor of justice, law, and society at American University, and Sandra McGunigall-Smith is an associate professor of legal studies at Utah Valley University. In the following viewpoint, the authors make the case that life in prison without parole is "death by incarceration." Through research and interviews conducted with prisoners at Utah State Prison from 1997 to 2002, Johnson and McGunigall-Smith present statements from prisoners illustrating how life in prison sometimes is viewed as a fate worse than execution. Based on their research, Johnson and McGunigall-Smith conclude that life in prison without parole could effectively replace the death penalty.

As you read, consider the following questions:

1. To what do the authors say objections to replacing death by execution with death by incarceration relate?

Adapted from Robert Johnson and Sandra McGunigall-Smith, "Life Without Parole, America's Other Death Penalty," *The Prison Journal*, vol. 88 no. 2, June 2008, pp. 328–346. Copyright © 2008 by The Prison Journal. Reprinted by permission of SAGE.

2. What are "volunteers," according to the viewpoint?

3. What do the authors say is the most basic hurt inflicted by life without parole?

Life without parole is sometimes called a "true life sentence" because offenders are sentenced to spend the remainder of their natural lives in prison. A better term for this sentence might be *death by incarceration,* as these persons are, in effect, sentenced to die in prison. Indeed, it is argued here that the sentence of life in prison without the possibility of parole can be equally as painful as the death penalty, albeit in different ways. The sentence can thus be thought of as "our other death penalty."

Offenders sentenced to death by incarceration suffer a "civil death." Their freedom—the essential feature of our civil society—has come to a permanent end. These prisoners are physically alive, of course, but they live only in prison. It might be better to say they "exist" in prison, as prison life is but a pale shadow of life in the free world. Their lives are steeped in suffering. The prison is their cemetery, a cell their tomb. If we as a society were to limit life without parole to aggravated murders, as we try to do with capital punishment, it could be argued that lifers give their civil lives in return for the natural lives they have taken. Under this formulation, use of life sentences for crimes short of capital murder would be excessive and unjust. By the same token, capital punishment would be entirely unnecessary, as capital murder would be adequately punished by "our other death penalty," death by incarceration.

Objections to replacing death by execution with death by incarceration relate to public safety (e.g., are lifers a danger to others in prison or the outside world?) and adequacy of punishment (e.g., is a life sentence sufficient punishment for capital murder?). As we shall see, life without parole does not pose a special risk to public safety and is a sanction of great severity, arguably comparable to the death sentence in the suffering it entails. Moreover, it is worth noting that one of the unique features of death by incarceration is that it allows a large window of time—much larger than that afforded by the death penalty—for evidence of innocence to emerge and thus permits the release and perhaps compensation of persons wrongly sentenced to prison for life. . . .

Some Prisoners Say a Life Sentence Is Worse than a Death Sentence

Life sentence inmates are manageable prisoners, some are even model prisoners, but their decent adjustment does not change the fact that their lives are marked by suffering and privation. Lifers do not adjust well because prison life is easy; they adjust well because self-interest moves them to make the most of a very difficult situation—a life confined to the barren, demeaning, and often dangerous world of the prison.

Some of us fail to appreciate the rigors of a life in prison because we do not believe prison is punishment. Prisoners are given a roof over their heads, three meals a day, and basic amenities like showers, recreation periods, and even ready access to television. Some prisons are air-conditioned. Because prisoners do not have to work to be fed, clothed, and housed, it may appear—even to the inmates themselves—that they are being coddled. But the deeper reality is emotional, not physical, and it is the emotional aspects of prison life that inmates find enormously stressful. As one inmate told McGunigall-Smith:

> It may sound weird but the actual physical part of being here is really easy. It almost makes you feel like you're a baby because you're fed, all you're bills are taken care of. You don't have to do anything. You don't have to get out of bed in the morning if you don't want to. . . . Everything is provided. But, the emotional is hard. I hate this place with a passion. I cannot stand it. Sometimes I wake up and start

looking around me and then I just lay there with my eyes closed because I just don't want to look at it. I don't want to see the concrete. I don't want to remember that I'm here.

One source of evidence on the extent of pain associated with a life sentence is provided by condemned prisoners who tell us point-blank that a life sentence is worse than a death sentence. These are not just empty words. A remarkable 123 prisoners—11% of the 1,099 executions carried out at the time of this writing [June 2008]—have dropped their appeals and allowed themselves to be killed. Some of these "volunteers," as they are sometimes called, lived on death rows that afforded more liberties and comforts than many maximum-security prisons. In Utah, for example, death row inmates with clean disciplinary records (which is true for the majority of condemned prisoners) have up to 6 hours out of the cell, during which time they can mingle with one another freely. They may have televisions (if they can afford to pay for them) in their air-conditioned cells. When Joseph Parsons, a Utah prisoner, dropped his appeals and was executed in 1999, his aim was not to get away from oppressive death row conditions. He wanted to get away from prison entirely, not just death row. Parsons made it quite clear that he preferred death in the execution chamber to life in prison: "I think it takes more courage to go on." In his view, "dying is easy . . . it takes guts to keep plodding along."

In prison, Parsons made clear, "plodding along" means living an empty, futile existence. Visibly weary of life in prison, Parsons observed:

> There has to be something better than this. Nothing could be worse than this. I'm not a religious person—I'm not into God and all that and the Devil and all that stuff. But if you want to use a good analogy this has got to be hell right here. There can't be anything worse than this. What they say is hell, the fire burning, the torture and everything else, well at least you're doing something! Here . . . it doesn't make any sense to me.

A Death Row Inmate Seeks Execution to Avoid Life in Prison

Six hours before he was executed, Parsons was asked about his feelings about his impending execution. He replied, "I'm not scared about the time between now and my execution. It's easy. The hard part is living every day here." Asked if he had second thoughts, he replied emphatically, "Have I had second thoughts? No. I'm tired of being here." Remarkably, Parsons was eager to face execution:

> I'm looking forward to this. The situation I'm in now is horrible. To me, I can't think of anything worse than this . . . to me, in my situation that I am in right now, this is the worst it could possibly be so it's a relief to know that I'm not going to be here no more . . . the next journey has got to be better than this one. All my bad karma came and hit me hard in this lifetime. I believe in good karma and bad karma. I got to figure in the next one I'm going to have a chance to do a little bit of good.

Parsons never maintained that the physical conditions of his confinement were what drove him to drop his appeals. As he told McGunigall-Smith "we've got three meals a day. We got a TV and a radio. We got air-conditioning in summer (sometimes)." His life was hell in part because of the other people around him. Like [French existentialist philosopher and playwright Jean-Paul] Sartre, he found hell in the fact that there was "no exit" [Sartre wrote a play called *No Exit*] from the company of people he held in contempt, some of whom (both inmates and guards) he characterized as "idiots." More important, Parsons stressed that he was never treated as a person, which is to say, shown respect and concern during incarceration. His degrading treatment was vividly brought home to him when he was sent to a civilian hospital for emergency surgery. His treatment there was in sharp contrast to his treatment as a death row prisoner:

The hospital staff were good to me, and their attitude was that I was a regular patient. They were pretty nice to me actually. Being able to get up and walk around was what made me feel real good. They were talking ... with me and making me laugh. ... I was walking around the halls talking to people. It kind of felt like I was a human being. I almost felt like I was normal.

It should be noted that Parsons was under very close supervision by prison staff during his stay at the hospital. The freedom he experienced was psychological, not physical. Because he was treated like a person, he felt free of the prison and therefore felt like a normal human being, not a captive. Back in prison, Parsons felt once again as he had always felt— that he was not seen as normal, not treated as a human being.

Parsons reports that he was always attuned to the various indignities and slights of prison life, which he claims were forcefully brought home to him by inconsistencies in the implementation of prison rules and procedures. These inconsistencies, in turn, interfered with his personal daily routine, disrupting his life and highlighting his sharply limited autonomy. Parsons stressed that he was "tired to death" of inconsistency. He was disturbed by schedules that changed in small ways but nevertheless in ways he could not anticipate and plan for; he resented promises by staff that were not kept or were left pending for longer than he could bear, leaving him on edge. To survive, Parsons needed a firm daily routine in which to lose himself. What he found on death row were small but repeated departures from routine that left him anxious and uncertain.

Parallels Exist Between Life Sentences and Death Sentences

For Parsons, life on death row was a precarious and exhausting battle to establish and maintain a routine with which he could live. More specifically, he sought a routine in which he

Life Without Parole Is a Sensible Alternative to the Death Penalty

The death penalty costs more, delivers less, and puts innocent lives at risk. Life without parole provides swift, severe, and certain punishment. It provides justice to survivors of murder victims and allows more resources to be invested into solving other murders and preventing violence.

"The Truth About Life Without Parole:
Condemned to Die in Prison," American Civil Liberties Union
(ACLU) of Northern California, 2011. www.aclunc.org.

could lose himself and not have to think about the indignity of a life lived in a place where he would never be a full-fledged human being, where he would never be treated as truly normal. Eventually, he simply ran out of energy. "I guess you have to deal with whoever and whatever comes in here," Parsons told McGunigall-Smith, "[but] I'm not dealing with it anymore. I'm tired of dealing with it." The sheer effort of trying to forge a routine strong enough to allow him to live by habit, free from painful introspection, was too much for him. "Even if it did change drastically," Parsons observed, "I wouldn't change my mind. I'm already dead." Death in the execution chamber looked better, much better, than life in prison as Parsons had come to know it.

Lifers, like Parsons and other execution volunteers, see many parallels between life sentences and death sentences. The lifers interviewed by McGunigall-Smith were asked which sentence they would prefer, a death sentence or a life sentence without the possibility of parole. The lifers were divided—eight chose the death penalty, eight chose life without parole (their current sentence), and six were ambivalent, sometimes preferring execution, at other times preferring life in prison. Typical of those who would choose death is the sentiment that life in prison is an exercise in futility. "Despite my best efforts," observed one lifer, "I lead a pointless, monastic existence with no end in sight.... I live in hell." Note that this concern for a pointless, empty life, a kind of living hell from an existential point of view, is exactly what motivated Parsons to drop his appeals and hasten his execution.

Prisoners who chose life sentences did so, to paraphrase a common view, because where there is life, there is hope—for release. Nothing about prison life offered any intrinsic appeal; the goal of choosing life in prison was to achieve the extrinsic goal of release from prison. Prisoners who expressed ambivalence about which was worse, life in prison or death in the execution chamber, framed the choice as a struggle with two more or less equally unappealing options. Said one prisoner, "there are times when I think I would be better off [executed] just because we're not doing nothing at all [here in prison]." Another man described an emotional journey in which an original preference for execution gave way to a grudging embrace of life in prison because prison life offered more pain, not less:

> In the beginning I did [want the death penalty]. I was feeling sorry for myself because I got caught. The death penalty, in my mind at that time, would have erased everything. I would have ceased to exist. The pain would cease. As time went by, I grew to enjoy that pain. That pain woke me up. To me the death penalty is the easy way out.

To call the death penalty "the easy way out" does not, in our view, minimize the pains of life under sentence of death by execution. Life on death row may well be a kind of psychological torture, as suggested by Parsons and supported in some research, but death row prisoners like Parsons have the legally valid choice to end that torturous existence by dropping their appeals and submitting to the judgment of the court. Lifers have no comparable choice; the life sentence offers prisoners no legal way to end their suffering. Life in prison had been chosen for them and indeed imposed on them by the courts, and in this sense, their life sentences render them less autonomous than condemned prisoners. . . .

The most basic hurt inflicted by life without parole is this: a lifetime of boredom, doubt, and anxiety punctuated by piercing moments of insight into one's failings as a human being. As one inmate told McGunigall-Smith, "my life is ruined for life; there is no redemption, and to some that is a fate worse than death." This miserable existence only ends when the prisoner dies—alone, unmourned, a disgrace in the person's own eyes as well as in the eyes of society.

If our goal is to make prisoners suffer greatly for the rest of their lives, life imprisonment without the possibility of parole offers itself as perhaps the ultimate punishment we can inflict. If our goal is justice, the bedrock principle of proportionality in punishment requires that we reserve this ultimate punishment for the ultimate crime: capital murder. Once we accept death by incarceration as our ultimate legal sanction, moreover, we should provide to all defendants facing this sanction the same legal safeguards and appellate procedures presently afforded to capital defendants. The oft-heard refrain that "death is different" explains the special attention to procedure in capital trials and subsequent appellate review. Death by incarceration is different as well. Our research leads us to conclude that death by incarceration is just as final, just as painful, and just as worthy of the careful scrutiny to which we subject traditional capital sentences.

Periodical and Internet Sources Bibliography

The following articles have been selected to supplement the diverse views presented in this chapter.

Pascal Calogero Jr.	"We Need Reforms to Increase Confidence in the Justice System," *The Times-Picayune* (New Orleans), February 29, 2012.
Andrew Cohen	"The Looming Death of the Death Penalty," *Atlantic*, December 15, 2011.
Charles W. Hoffman	"Abolishing Death Penalty Was Right Choice for State," *Chicago Sun-Times*, March 4, 2012.
John Horgan	"History Suggests the U.S. Will Ban the Death Penalty Soon. Why Not Now?," *Scientific American*, September 26, 2011.
Patrik Jonsson	"Troy Davis Execution Protest Confronts Support for Death Penalty," *Christian Science Monitor*, September 24, 2011.
Los Angeles Times	"First, Abolish the Death Penalty: The So-Called SAFE California Act's Goal of Abolishing the Death Penalty Is the Right One," March 12, 2012.
New York Times	"The Misuse of Life Without Parole," September 12, 2011.
Dennis Prager	"If You're Ever Murdered . . . ," *National Review Online*, February 21, 2012. www.nationalreview.com.
Jonathan Simon	"The Paradoxical Status of 'Life Without Parole,'" *The Berkeley Blog*, September 15, 2011. http://blogs.berkeley.edu.
Washington Post	"Maryland's Broken Death Penalty," March 6, 2012.

For Further Discussion

Chapter 1

1. Considering the viewpoints in this chapter, do you think it is possible for the death penalty to be legal but not ethical or just? On the other hand, is it possible for the death penalty to be ethical or just but not legal? What accounts for these differences, and what or who should the final authority be when it comes to deciding such matters?

2. In this chapter, there is some discussion about human rights as they relate to the death penalty. Does someone who commits murder or a serious crime forfeit (voluntarily give up) their rights—including their right to life and humane treatment? In protecting the rights of innocent, law-abiding citizens, is it necessary that those who commit the worst crimes pay with their lives? Why or why not? If not, what are some alternatives?

Chapter 2

1. The question of whether the death penalty deters crime and saves lives is examined in the viewpoint written by David Muhlhausen. In addition to this viewpoint are conflicting studies about the deterrent effect that the death penalty has on crime rates. Some studies show that it is effective in lowering crime, while other research seems to indicate that it has little effect. Without clear data proving the deterrent effect of the death penalty, should it continue to be used as a punishment? Why or why not? Is it necessary that punishment for society's worst crimes have a deterrent effect? If not, what is the primary goal of punishing society's worst criminals?

2. According to the viewpoint written by Julie Delcour, the average cost of one death penalty case—from arrest to execution—can run between $1 to $3 million. Yet according to a 2008 poll of police chiefs nationwide, many said they believed that the death penalty was the least efficient use of taxpayer dollars and that, in their opinion, it did not deter homicides. In light of financial challenges and budget cuts facing many states, what are some actions that government officials can take to lower costs, and should states consider abolishing the death penalty on the basis of cost alone? Should there be limits set on how much is spent on death penalty cases and in overall efforts to deter crime? If so, how should those limits be determined?

Chapter 3

1. The subject of racial bias within the death penalty system is discussed in viewpoints written by David A. Love and Charles Lane. Both have a different perspective on the progress that has been made in eliminating racial bias from the death penalty system. Given the information presented in both viewpoints—and considering some of the reforms mentioned as a result of court cases in recent years—is it possible to completely eliminate bias from the death penalty system? If not, why not? If it is not possible to administer the death penalty in a fair, unbiased way, should it continue to be used as a form of punishment? Explain.

2. Based on Radley Balko's viewpoint, DNA testing has raised serious questions about how many people have been wrongfully convicted of crimes. Given the information presented in this viewpoint and in the one written by Juan Roberto Meléndez-Colón, how is it possible that an innocent person might be sitting on death row? And if

DNA testing is unable to prevent wrongful convictions, as Meléndez-Colón points out, what can be done to prevent them?

3. In this chapter, there is some discussion about exempting those who have severe mental illness from the death penalty. What is the rationale behind this idea, and what role should society play—if any—in protecting those who are mentally impaired, either by mental illness or mental retardation? If someone who is mentally impaired commits a crime, how should society respond as it relates to punishment? Where the mentally ill are concerned, what preventive measures can be taken before a crime is committed?

Chapter 4

1. Mario M. Cuomo argues that the death penalty is wrong on many different levels and is an ineffective punishment that should be abolished. Bruce Fein, on the other hand, argues that some crimes are so morally abhorrent and despicable that only the death penalty is adequate punishment for them. Which author do you feel presents the more persuasive argument, and why? Cite examples from the viewpoints to support your reasoning.

2. Robert Johnson and Sandra McGunigall-Smith say that life in prison without parole is "death by incarceration." What do they mean by this? Is life in prison without parole as effective a punishment as the death penalty, based on what you have read in their viewpoint? Why or why not?

Organizations to Contact

The editors have compiled the following list of organizations concerned with the issues debated in this book. The descriptions are derived from materials provided by the organizations. All have publications or information available for interested readers. The list was compiled on the date of publication of the present volume; the information provided here may change. Be aware that many organizations take several weeks or longer to respond to inquiries, so allow as much time as possible.

American Civil Liberties Union (ACLU)
125 Broad Street, 18th Floor, New York, NY   10004
(212) 549-2500 • fax: (212) 549-2646
e-mail: aclu@aclu.org
website: www.aclu.org

The American Civil Liberties Union (ACLU) believes that capital punishment violates the Constitution's ban on cruel and unusual punishment as well as the requirements of due process and equal protection under the law. Its Capital Punishment Project is dedicated to abolishing the death penalty. The ACLU maintains the *Blog of Rights* and publishes numerous books and pamphlets, including "The Case Against the Death Penalty."

Amnesty International USA
5 Penn Plaza, New York, NY   10001
(212) 807-8400 • fax: (212) 627-1451
e-mail: aimember@aiusa.org
website: www.amnestyusa.org

Amnesty International USA's Abolish the Death Penalty campaign seeks the abolishment of the death penalty worldwide. Its most recent activities have been aimed at decreasing the use of the death penalty internationally, including in the United States, and increasing the number of countries that have removed the death penalty as an option for punishment. It also serves as an advocate in individual clemency cases. Amnesty International USA publishes news, fact sheets, and reports, including "The Death Penalty Resource Guide" and "Amnesty International Debates the Death Penalty."

Campaign to End the Death Penalty (CEDP)

PO Box 25730, Chicago, IL   60625
(773) 955-4841 • fax: (773) 955-4842
website: www.nodeathpenalty.org

The Campaign to End the Death Penalty (CEDP) is a national grassroots organization dedicated to the abolition of capital punishment in the United States. Its website contains local contact information, regular updates on death row cases, and fact sheets about capital punishment in the United States. CEDP regularly publishes a newsletter, *The New Abolitionist*.

Catholics Against Capital Punishment (CACP)

PO Box 5706, Bethesda, MD   20824-5706
fax: (301) 654-0925
e-mail: ellen.frank@verizon.net
website: www.cacp.org

Founded in 1992 to promote the Catholic Church's teachings about capital punishment, Catholics Against Capital Punishment (CACP) is a national organization that works to stop the death penalty in the United States. The organization's newsletter, *CACP News Notes*, is published four to six times a year.

Criminal Justice Legal Foundation (CJLF)

2131 L Street, Sacramento, CA   95816
(916) 446-0345
website: www.cjlf.org

The Criminal Justice Legal Foundation (CJLF) was established in 1982 as a nonprofit, public interest law organization dedicated to restoring a balance between the rights of crime victims and the accused. The CJLF sponsors the blog *Crime & Consequences*, and its website offers links to various transcripts, articles, and working papers, including "The Death Penalty and Plea Bargaining to Life Sentences."

Death Penalty Information Center (DPIC)
1015 Eighteenth Street NW, Suite 704, Washington, DC   20036
(202) 289-2275 • fax: (202) 289-7336
website: www.deathpenaltyinfo.org

The Death Penalty Information Center (DPIC) opposes the death penalty because it believes that capital punishment is discriminatory, costly to taxpayers, and may result in innocent persons being put to death. Its website publishes public opinion reports, testimony, and news articles about public views on the death penalty, including "Smart on Crime: Reconsidering the Death Penalty in a Time of Economic Crisis" and "A Crisis of Confidence: Americans' Doubts About the Death Penalty."

Equal Justice Initiative (EJI)
122 Commerce Street, Montgomery, AL   36104
(334) 269-1803 • fax: (334) 269-1806
e-mail: contact_us@eji.org
website: www.eji.org

A nonprofit organization, the Equal Justice Initiative (EJI) provides legal representation to indigent defendants and prisoners who have been denied fair and just treatment in the legal system. EJI also prepares reports, newsletters, and manuals to assist advocates and policy makers in reforming the criminal justice system. Its website offers videos, news articles, and reports, including "Cruel and Unusual: Sentencing 13- and 14-Year-Old Children to Die in Prison."

Innocence Project
40 Worth Street, Suite 701, New York, NY   10013
(212) 364-5340

e-mail: info@innocenceproject.org
website: www.innocenceproject.org

The Innocence Project is dedicated to exonerating wrongfully convicted people through DNA testing and reforming the criminal justice system to prevent future injustice. As of July 2008, it has assisted in the exoneration of 218 people in the United States, each of whom served an average of twelve years in prison, including sixteen who served time on death row. The Innocence Project publishes the *Innocence Blog*, monthly e-newsletters, fact sheets, and reports, including "Lineups: Why Witnesses Make Mistakes and How to Reduce the Chance of a Misidentification."

Justice Fellowship
44180 Riverside Parkway, Lansdowne, VA   20176
(877) 478-0100
e-mail: justicefellowship@pfm.org
website: www.justicefellowship.org

The Justice Fellowship is a Christian organization that bases its work for reform of the justice system on the concept of victim-offender reconciliation. It does not take a position on the death penalty. On its website, the fellowship publishes true stories of restoration as well as the "Justice eReport" and other commentary and reports, including "Capital Punishment: A Call to Dialogue" and "Monitoring Death Sentencing Decisions: The Challenges and Barriers to Equity."

Justice for All
PO Box 55159, Houston, TX   77255
(713) 935-9300 • fax: (713) 935-9301
e-mail: info@jfa.net
website: www.jfa.net

Justice for All is an all-volunteer, nonprofit criminal justice reform organization that supports the death penalty. Its activities include publishing the monthly newsletter *The Voice of Justice* and circulating online petitions to keep violent offenders from being paroled early.

Lincoln Institute for Research and Education

PO Box 254, Great Falls, VA 22066
(703) 759-4278 • fax: (703) 759-4597
e-mail: contactus@lincolnreview.com
website: www.lincolnreview.com

The Lincoln Institute for Research and Education is a conservative think tank that studies public policy issues affecting the lives of black Americans, including the issue of the death penalty, which the institute favors. It publishes commentary, amicus briefs, and the *Lincoln Letter Review*.

National Coalition to Abolish the Death Penalty

1705 DeSales Street NW, Fifth Floor, Washington, DC 20036
(202) 331-4090
website: www.ncadp.org

The National Coalition to Abolish the Death Penalty is a collection of more than one hundred groups working together to stop executions in the United States and throughout the world. The organization compiles statistics on the death penalty. To further its goal, the coalition publishes blogs, information packets, pamphlets, research materials, and the quarterly newsletter *LifeLines*.

National Criminal Justice Reference Service (NCJRS)

PO Box 6000, Rockville, MD 20849-6000
(301) 519-5500 • fax: (301) 519-5212
website: www.ncjrs.gov

Established in 1972, the National Criminal Justice Reference Service (NCJRS) is a federally funded resource offering justice information to support research, policy, and program development worldwide. NCJRS hosts one of the largest criminal and juvenile justice libraries and databases in the world. Among its many publications are the biweekly electronic newsletter *JUSTINFO* and the report "Justice Delayed? Time Consumption in Capital Appeals: A Multistate Study."

United States Department of Justice
950 Pennsylvania Avenue NW, Washington, DC   20530-0001
(202) 514-2000
e-mail: AskDOJ@usdoj.gov
website: www.usdoj.gov

The mission of the Department of Justice is to enforce US law, provide federal leadership in preventing and controlling crime, seek just punishment for those guilty of unlawful behavior, and ensure fair and impartial administration of justice for all Americans. Its website publishes press releases, *The Justice Blog*, and various reports, including "Capital Punishment Statistical Tables."

Bibliography of Books

Sanaz Alasti — *Cruel and Unusual Punishment: Comparative Perspective in International Conventions, the United States and Iran*. Lake Mary, FL: Vandeplas Publishing, 2009.

Howard W. Allen, Jerome M. Clubb, and Vincent A. Lacey — *Race, Class, and the Death Penalty: Capital Punishment in American History*. Albany: State University of New York Press, 2008.

Robert Badinter — *Abolition: One Man's Battle Against the Death Penalty*. Boston, MA: Northeastern University Press, 2008.

Frank R. Baumgartner, Suzanna L. De Boef, and Amber E. Boydstun — *The Decline of the Death Penalty and the Discovery of Innocence*. New York: Cambridge University Press, 2008.

Elizabeth Beck, Sarah Britto, and Arlene Andrews — *In the Shadow of Death: Restorative Justice and Death Row Families*. New York: Oxford University Press, 2007.

Hugo Adam Bedau and Paul G. Cassell, eds. — *Debating the Death Penalty: Should America Have Capital Punishment? The Experts on Both Sides Make Their Best Case*. New York: Oxford University Press, 2004.

Christopher Berry-Dee and Tony Brown — *Dead Men Walking: True Stories of the Most Evil Men and Women on Death Row*. London: John Blake Publishing Ltd., 2008.

John D. Bessler   *Cruel & Unusual: The American Death Penalty and the Founders' Eighth Amendment.* Boston, MA: Northeastern University Press, 2012.

Robert M. Bohm   *DeathQuest: An Introduction to the Theory and Practice of Capital Punishment in the United States.* 4th ed. Cincinnati, OH: Anderson Publishing Co., 2012.

Robert M. Bohm   *Ultimate Sanction: Understanding the Death Penalty Through Its Many Voices and Many Sides.* New York: Kaplan Publishing, 2010.

Raymond Bonner   *Anatomy of Injustice: A Murder Case Gone Wrong.* New York: Alfred A. Knopf, 2012.

Michael Dow Burkhead   *A Life for a Life: The American Debate over the Death Penalty.* Jefferson, NC: McFarland & Co., 2009.

Thomas Cahill   *A Saint on Death Row: The Story of Dominique Green.* New York: Doubleday Publishing, 2009.

Bill Crawford   *Texas Death Row: Executions in the Modern Era.* New York: Plume, 2008.

D.D. de Vinci   *Dead Family Walking: The Bourque Family Story of Dead Man Walking.* New Iberia, LA: Goldlamp Publishing, 2005.

David R. Dow   *The Autobiography of an Execution.* New York: Twelve, 2010.

David Garland	*Peculiar Institution: America's Death Penalty in an Age of Abolition.* Cambridge, MA: Belknap Press of Harvard University Press, 2010.
David Garland, Randall McGowen, and Michael Meranze, eds.	*America's Death Penalty: Between Past and Present.* New York: NYU Press, 2011.
Brandon L. Garrett	*Convicting the Innocent: Where Criminal Prosecutions Go Wrong.* Cambridge, MA: Harvard University Press, 2011.
Rudolph J. Gerber and John M. Johnson	*The Top Ten Death Penalty Myths: The Politics of Crime Control.* Westport, CT: Praeger, 2007.
Norma Herrera	*Last Words from Death Row: The Walls Unit.* Mequon, WI: Nightengale Press, 2007.
Bruce Jackson and Diane Christian	*In This Timeless Time: Living and Dying on Death Row in America.* Chapel Hill: University of North Carolina Press, 2012.
Richard S. Jaffe	*Quest for Justice: Defending the Damned.* Far Hills, NJ: New Horizon Press, 2012.
Charles Lane	*Stay of Execution: Saving the Death Penalty from Itself.* Lanham, MD: Rowman & Littlefield, 2010.

Charles S. Lanier, William J. Bowers, and James R. Acker, eds.

The Future of America's Death Penalty: An Agenda for the Next Generation of Capital Punishment Research. Durham, NC: Carolina Academic Press, 2009.

Barry Latzer and David McCord

Death Penalty Cases: Leading U.S. Supreme Court Cases on Capital Punishment. 3rd ed. Burlington, MA: Butterworth-Heinemann, 2011.

Andrea D. Lyon

Angel of Death Row: My Life as a Death Penalty Defense Lawyer. New York: Kaplan Publishing, 2010.

Brian MacQuarrie

The Ride: A Shocking Murder and a Bereaved Father's Journey from Rage to Redemption. Cambridge, MA: Da Capo Press, 2009.

Jarvis Jay Masters

That Bird Has My Wings: The Autobiography of an Innocent Man on Death Row. New York: HarperCollins, 2009.

Russell G. Murphy

Voices of the Death Penalty Debate: A Citizen's Guide to Capital Punishment. Lake Mary, FL: Vandeplas Publishing, 2010.

David M. Oshinsky

Capital Punishment on Trial: Furman v. Georgia and the Death Penalty in Modern America. Lawrence, KS: University Press of Kansas, 2010.

Mark William Osler

Jesus on Death Row: The Trial of Jesus and American Capital Punishment. Nashville, TN: Abingdon Press, 2009.

Raymond Paternoster, Robert Brame, and Sarah Bacon	*The Death Penalty: America's Experience with Capital Punishment.* New York: Oxford University Press, 2008.
Carroll Pickett with Carlton Stowers	*Within These Walls: Memoirs of a Death House Chaplain.* New York: St. Martin's Press, 2002.
Helen Prejean	*The Death of Innocents: An Eyewitness Account of Wrongful Executions.* New York: Random House, 2005.
Dale S. Recinella	*The Biblical Truth About America's Death Penalty.* Boston, MA: Northeastern University Press, 2004.
Wilbert Rideau	*In the Place of Justice: A Story of Punishment and Deliverance.* New York: Alfred A. Knopf, 2010.
Austin Sarat	*Mercy on Trial: What It Means to Stop an Execution.* Princeton, NJ: Princeton University Press, 2007.
Scott Turow	*Ultimate Punishment: A Lawyer's Reflections on Dealing with the Death Penalty.* New York: Farrar, Straus, and Giroux, 2003.
Thomas G. Walker	*Eligible for Execution: The Story of the Daryl Atkins Case.* Washington, DC: CQ Press, 2008.

Index